'50s & '60s
STYLE

POLLY POWELL & LUCY PEEL

JG PRESS

A QUINTET BOOK

Published in the USA 1996 by JG Press.
Distributed by World Publications, Inc.

The JG Press imprint is a trademark of
JG Press, Inc.
455 Somerset Avenue
North Dighton, MA 02764

This edition produced for sale in the USA, its
territories and dependencies only.

ISBN 1-57215-172-2

This book was designed and produced by
Quintet Publishing Limited
6 Blundell Street
London N7 9BH

Art Director: Peter Bridgewater
Designer: Ian Hunt
Editors: Paul Barnett and Judith Simons
Picture Researcher: Kate Duffy
Illustrator: Annie Ellis

Typeset in Great Britain by
Central Southern Typesetters, Eastbourne
Manufactured in Hong Kong by
Regent Publishing Services Limited
Printed in Singapore by
Star Standard Industries (Pte) Ltd

ACKNOWLEDGEMENTS
The authors and publishers would like to thank
Alexander Garett for his contribution on graphic
design and Geoffrey Powell for his contribution on
architecture. They would also like to thank
Robert Opie of the Museum of Advertising and
Packaging in Gloucester for supplying many of the
illustrations.

Contents

’50s & ’60s Style Preview

1960—1965

1966—1969

GIs and ATS girls. The war enforced contact between people of different cultures and classes, and, during the post-war years, global cultural and market frontiers were to open, fostering a fertile exchange of ideas, talent and ethics.

SETTING THE STYLE

The Post-War Years

The two decades following World War II were a time of unprecedented social change. The state of war had necessitated radical revisions of people's roles in society – for example, women had had to take on work traditionally regarded as being strictly a male preserve – and the corresponding changes in popular attitudes persisted into peacetime. Out of this turmoil came the seeds of a new optimism that would eventually flower as the individualism and self-awareness, the sexual freedom and search for spiritual fulfilment that characterized the 1960s.

As the lights came on throughout Europe at the end of the war they illuminated not just bunting and flags but also cities laid waste by bombs, impassable roads, blocked canals and the ruins of bridges and railways. The industrial centres – what was left of them – had given over all their manufacturing capacity to the war effort, and it was clear that it would take many years and a great deal of money and effort to put Europe back on its feet and get the factories producing consumer goods again.

The war had turned Europe into a melting pot. It gave ordinary people the chance to travel – albeit in conditions that were far from deluxe! British and Australasian soldiers went to Europe, Africa, India and the Far East, and North Americans to Europe and the Pacific. It brought the rich into factories and country dwellers into the towns, while uncounted evacuees made the opposite journey, from the cities out into rural areas. Refugees fled to 'new' countries. The effect of all this was to bring people of different cultures and classes into direct contact in a way unthinkable before the war.

This mixing of circumstances made people realize the inequalities of living standards that had hitherto existed, and the masses became hungry for change. A cry went up for a 'new world' and 'prosperity for all'. Probably the most important product of this changed world-view was the welfare state. It took different forms in different countries. In Britain a full contributory system was established, while in Italy, Austria and the Netherlands the schemes introduced involved a combination of state and private insurance; some countries, such as the United States, France, Germany and Spain, set up a rudimentary 'safety net' service. Yet, however minimal the provision in a particular nation, it was enough to give people a sense of security and to lay the foundations of the affluent society.

The United States, on the other hand, had not fared too badly during the war, which if anything had stimulated the country's economy, making it the greatest power on earth – with all

the responsibilities which that entailed. No longer could it pursue its pre-war isolationist policies. The United States showed it was taking its duties seriously with the introduction, in April 1948, of the Marshall Plan, designed to put Europe back on its feet through the provision of US aid and loans. This signalled the start of an interdependence between the United States and Western Europe that went far beyond the exchange of goods to include a cross-fertilization of ideas, culture and talent.

The dark side of the post-war period was the growth of hostility, suspicion and fear between the communist countries of the East – primarily the USSR and its satellites, the 'Iron Curtain' countries – and the democracies and pseudo-democracies generally lumped together as 'the West'. Any hopes for a united world evaporated after the Yalta and Potsdam conferences of 1945, when a series of broken promises by Stalin made the West realize that it had virtually given away Eastern Europe and in so doing had created a monster, the 'Eastern Bloc'. That, added to the fear that the USSR might get 'the Bomb' and the Berlin Crisis of 1948–9, spawned the Cold War and a paranoid fear of communism that in the 1950s erupted in the United States in the form of McCarthyism, and shaped many Western countries' foreign policies during the 1950s and 1960s.

■ **Opposite above** The wartime arrival of GIs in the UK gave many British people a glimpse of the good life being enjoyed across the Atlantic.

■ **Opposite below** World War II displaced millions of people throughout the world and turned Europe into a melting pot.

■ **Top** Blanket bombing left numerous cities devastated. It was to take a great deal of effort and money to put Europe back on its feet.

■ **Above** VE Day in London: once the bunting and flags had been cleared away the job of reconstruction had to begin.

2000 coffee set, designed by Raymond Loewy and Richard Latham in 1954, and manufactured by Rosenthal.

1950-1954

Into the Future

The 1950s started on a high note. People believed that they were entering a new age in which *anything* was possible. Indeed, there seemed to be no limits to humanity's potential for achievement. In science, a vaccine against polio was just around the corner, atomic power had been harnessed to make electricity (advertised in the United States by a woman frying 'Atomburgers' outside a power station!), the structure of DNA had been identified, and radioisotopes came into general use in medicine and industry. The belief in benign technology was echoed in design and art through the portrayal of the molecular structures inferred by scientists – notably the double helix of DNA, which appeared as a motif in pictures, graphic designs and sculptures.

Other barriers fell. In Britain the Conservative Party under Winston Churchill won the 1951 General Election on the platform of prosperity for all and the promise that they would 'set the people free'. The 1951 Festival of Britain provided a much-needed boost to the country, and patriotic fervour reached fever pitch with the coronation of Queen Elizabeth II in 1953.

The newly formed welfare states in Europe promised freedom from want – the slogan used in Britain was 'security from the cradle to the grave'. Throughout Europe people began to look forward to an end to austerity and the beginning of prosperity, and they turned their attentions westward, to the United States, which they saw as embodying their new-found ideals of consumerism.

The Marshall Plan had put Europe on the road to recovery, but more work was needed. There was still a shortage of many essential goods;

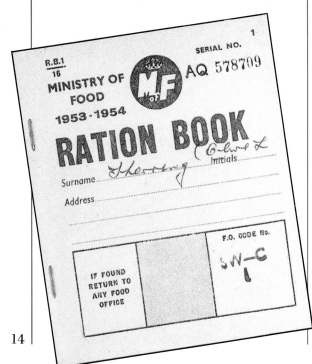

COMMUNIST PARTY ORGANIZATION U.S.A-FEB. 9, 1950

■ **Far left** With industry concentrating on reconstruction, production of consumer goods took second place. Thus rationing continued into the early 1950s.

■ **Left** The coronation of Queen Elizabeth II in 1953 provided the British with a much-needed distraction from the drabness of post-war austerity.

■ **Above** Senator Joseph McCarthy's Communist witch-hunts created a climate of fear and mistrust in the United States which spread from the army to Hollywood.

■ **Top** Security from the cradle to the grave was the promise of the new welfare systems in Europe.

rationing of some items continued into the early 1950s. In Britain, Italy, France, Germany and the Netherlands whole towns had to be rebuilt, a fabulous opportunity for architects and town planners, and industry had to be revived – planned on an international scale using the latest production-line techniques.

People believed they could build a brave new world from the ruins left by the war, but in the case of the conquered nations they had to restore more than buildings or economies – they had to restore pride and morale. Japan, for example, had been particularly devastated by the war. Its Samurai code had fostered the belief that it was infinitely superior to the West, and so its defeat and subsequent US occupation (until 1952) left it sapped of confidence and strength and open to

manipulation by the United States – which felt it needed a reliable Pacific ally as a hedge against the communism spreading throughout the Far East.

The tension between East and West was escalating, reaching high points with the Korean War in 1950 and the election of Dwight D. Eisenhower as US president in 1952. The 'Reds under the bed' paranoia was personified in the United States by Senator Joseph McCarthy, whose witch hunts – which started in the State Department and spread to Hollywood and the cultural and artistic community – caused a general atmosphere of distrust and fear. Further paranoia was fuelled by a series of spy scandals in Britain and the United States and by the USSR's testing of the atomic bomb in 1951 and the hydrogen bomb in 1953.

America at Home

Part of the great American Dream has always been a home for everyone, and during the 1950s this became possible. The advent of government-guaranteed mortgage funds for veterans as part of the GI Bill turned what had once seemed a fantasy into a reality. Through the Federal Housing Administration and Veterans' Association, ex-servicemen could buy a house without having to put down a deposit. 'No cash down for veterans' was the slogan on the posters advertising the newly built prefabricated 'tract' housing, and by 1957 40–50 per cent of houses sold were done so under these finance schemes. Altogether, ownership of single-family homes grew more in the decade of the 1950s than in the previous 150 years.

The houses the veterans bought were without exception part of the new suburbia built by such people as William Levitt. They came in four or five basic styles, ranging from 'Ranch' to 'Cape Cod', but were all fairly similar – and fairly basic. What the developers were trying to achieve (architects were not used) were open-plan single-storey or split-level houses with large picture windows looking out on to a lawn. Open-air living, typified by the informal barbecues, was the aim.

In their advertisements the developers laid great stress on the family and the community. Indeed, a massive baby boom took place during the early 1950s, due in part to the fact that couples were tending to get married younger. The ideal family comprised mother, father and two children, with the father going off to his job in the city every day while mother spent her time ferrying the children around between school, baseball practice, swimming lessons and so on. It was true that most women did not work, although the idea of the career woman was not utterly unheard of – as shown by an article in April 1950 in *Woman's Home Companion*, 'Do Women Really Want Outside Jobs?' Interestingly, the article reported the results of a poll which showed that 52 per cent of readers wanted to stay at home while the rest plumped for part-time jobs: the idea of a full-time career was not even considered.

Father's job in the city would more than likely be with a large corporation, and as a loyal and ambitious company man he would be expected to toe the line – even if this meant frequent moves to different parts of the country. By 1954 one in five US citizens moved house each year.

Because of the constantly shifting population, communities had little chance to grow in the suburbs. Also, young couples were separated early from their families, and so became very susceptible to advertising and the new media. For example, they would be more likely to look to Dr

Spock than to their parents for advice about their children, while television would be a major influence on their views of what was the norm.

By the end of the 1950s television was the single most important form of mass entertainment and culture. It spawned vast industries producing spin-offs, such as the ubiquitous 'TV dinner' – just one form of the new convenience foods that lined the shelves of the huge new supermarkets. Thanks to television, all-American families could sit in their modern suburban homes and watch sitcoms about other all-American families just like themselves. Through advertising, television also showed people a massive range of consumer goods just waiting to be bought, and soon what had been considered luxuries – such as the latest model of car or cooker – were deemed necessities.

■ **Above** The American dream of a home for everyone became reality with massive development of prefabricated 'tract' housing such as at Levittown, Long Island.

■ **Above right** Mother as homemaker: the new convenience foods provided a quick and easy way to provide those tasty treats for all the family.

■ **Far right** Informal barbecues were a vital part of the popular perception of the outdoor way of life.

■ **Right** Thanks to advertising, what had previously been deemed luxuries came to be considered necessities·

GREEN'S
'Carmellé

Greens 'Carmellé
WITH CARAMEL
TOPPING
INCLUDED
IT'S
NEW!

The Festival of Britain

The most important event to affect the design of mass-produced goods in Britain during the early 1950s was the Festival of Britain. For a time the 'Festival Style', as it became known, could be seen everywhere, from chairs and furnishing fabrics to magazine covers and ball-point pens. However, as the organizers of the exhibition later acknowledged, the designs on show – the inspirations behind the style – were hardly innovative. They were, in fact, the product of a generation of architects and designers who had been starved of commissions during World War II, and who were eager to realize schemes and ideas some of which had been percolating for over a decade. The Festival provided not only the opportunity for these architects and designers to actually build and design, but also the chance for their work to be seen by many millions of people.

The idea to stage an exhibition to commemorate the Great Exhibition of 1851 was first put forward to the then Labour government by the Royal Society of Arts. The government supported the project with the proviso that the Festival would have both to be international and to include trade in order to justify the expense. In March 1948 Gerald Barry was made Director-General of the project and Herbert Morrison (later dubbed 'Lord Festival') became the minister responsible to the Cabinet. Six months later the project had taken enough shape for the Executive Committee to announce to the press the rather ambiguous aim of the Festival: 'What the Land has made of the People, and what the People have made of themselves.'

The enormous task of 'styling' the Festival fell to the Design Group under the leadership of Sir Hugh Casson. Other members of the team were two architects, Ralph Tubbs and Misha Black, and two designers, James Holland and James Gardner (coordinator of the highly successful 'Britain Can Make It' exhibition held in 1946). Such was the diversity of their job that they were equally responsible for selecting Powell & Moya's Skylon structure as for choosing the cleaners' uniforms.

The main site for the exhibition was to be London's South Bank, with some pleasure gardens and a funfair located in Battersea. Smaller simultaneous exhibitions were planned for Belfast and Glasgow and touring exhibitions were to cover the country. In early 1949 the plans were finalized, and the South Bank revealed an informal grouping of buildings – a sharp contrast to the rigid formal arrangements of earlier exhibitions.

Whether the motives behind the staging of such a festival were grounded in political strategy, economic considerations or pure philanthropy,

■ **Opposite above** The Festival of Britain attracted millions of visitors, including many foreigners. Special Festival interpreters were appointed.

■ **Opposite below** On show in the pavilions were many thousands of designs and products. Some exhibits were frivolous, but in other cases people were seriously seeking investors.

■ **Right** The Festival symbol – seen here on an official guide – was designed by Abram Games. It appeared on just about every form of souvenir, from ashtrays to bath soap. The village of Detling in Kent even went to the trouble of carving the symbol out of a hillside on the North Downs.

■ **Far right** A novelty box depicting the main Festival site, on London's South Bank, and showing the Dome of Discovery and the Skylon.

■ **Below** Spectacular light shows at night stunned a nation more accustomed to blackouts and shortages. Even the Skylon lit up at night.

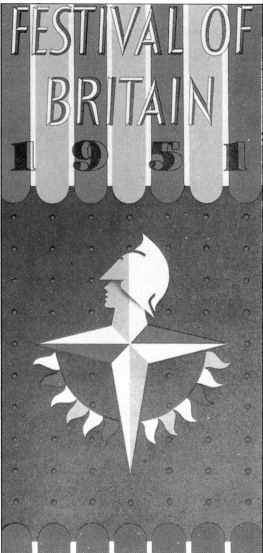

the outcome was very different from the original conception. By the time the turnstiles wound into action on 3 May 1951, it was neither international (it would have cost six times as much) and nor did it include trade (again, dropped for economic reasons). Furthermore, the exhibit to commemorate the Great Exhibition had almost been left out altogether. The Festival ended up with a less tangible but equally important purpose – that of nationalistic morale-boosting or, in the words of Gerald Barry, giving 'a tonic to the nation'.

The Festival stayed open for five months over the summer and was hugely successful: 8½ million people visited the South Bank to see the Dome of Discovery and the Skylon, and almost as many visited the pleasure gardens in Battersea. For a ration-weary public, the Festival must have represented everything that utility goods and austerity were not. The effect of the exhibition, and the Design Group in particular, on British design and 'Contemporary Style' in the immediate years was far-reaching, but in the end short-lived. As the writer Michael Frayn pointed out, 'the fashions it set in architecture and design were quickly copied, became clichés, and eventually looked vulgar against the growing affluence of the fifties'.

Molecular Patterns

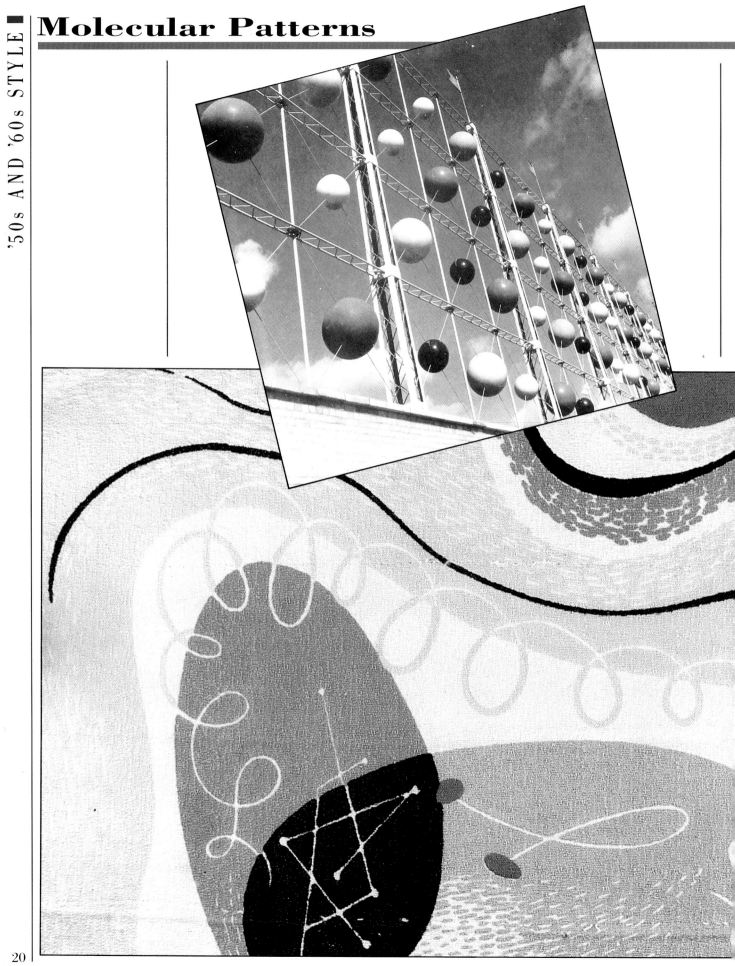

The 1950s saw tremendous advances in science, with the harnessing of atomic power to produce electricity, the use of radioisotopes in medicine and industry, and the discovery of the molecular structure of DNA. These breakthroughs were echoed in design with molecular patterns appearing on items as diverse as fabrics (**left**), lampshades (**above**) and magazine covers (**right**).

Top left The molecular theme figured prominently in the Festival of Britain, held in London in 1951, with constructions such as this huge screen.

Esquire

APRIL 1953

THE MAGAZINE FOR MEN

LET'S SECEDE FROM TEXAS
by Bernard Dorrity

LUCKY LUCIANO TALKS
by Leonard Lyons

Materials from the Lab

Many new materials which became popular in the 1950s were developed as substitutes during World War II as supplies of the real thing ran short. This was particularly true as far as textiles were concerned, for the conflict virtually halted the import of the raw materials used for their manufacture. But, by the end of the war, awareness was growing of the potential of the new materials in their own right, and an exhibition held in London in 1946, called 'Britain Can Make It', showed how industry could apply wartime military technology to peacetime domestic goods.

Some of the most important new materials to emerge were melamine, polyethylene, polystyrene and nylon. The last was possibly the one which most people came into contact with, for it was used for a wide variety of products ranging from the all-important stockings to hair spray.

The clothing industry was revolutionized by synthetic fibres. The new fabrics were easy to wash and drip-dry, and did not need to be ironed – improvements which reduced women's weekly laundry time by hours. Also, they allowed manufacturers to use a wider range of dyes to produce more vivid, even fluorescent, colours. The invention of Terylene (Dacron) allowed fabrics to be made that gave permanent 'knife' pleats to skirts and trousers. Orlon and Banlon, soft synthetic jersey materials, were used for body-hugging clothes such as the new tight stretch trousers, and rayon crêpe had the useful characteristic that it could be dyed as a fabric rather than as fibres. Stiffened nylon was made into huge petticoats which kept their shape without support and were very light. By the late 1950s most girls would have at least one in their wardrobes to wear with their circular skirts. There was much experimentation in the combination of natural and synthetic fibres. For example, Chinazano was a mixture of silk with Orlon, and had the crush-resistant qualities of manmade materials.

Furniture manufacturers made great use of the

■ **Right** The Marley Tile Company dominated the UK market with a range available in numerous colours and patterns.

■ **Opposite below right** New methods of finishing aluminium made it more appealing to consumers; soon aluminium objects were to be found even on the dining table.

WARM...YET LIGHT

Now—a jacket that's warm enough for the coldest weather, yet weighs only 21½ oz.! It's made of 100% Du Pont nylon

DU PONT NYLON
DUPONT

FORMICA for me!

■ **Left and right** Synthetic materials such as nylon were light, bright and drip-dry, and were used to make anything from jackets to stockings.

■ **Above** Formica came into its own in the 1950s, replacing enamel which had been used in the 1940s for tabletops.

new materials. Techniques of furniture construction could break radically with convention using methods such as moulding. For example, Eero Saarinen's 'tulip' series of chairs, made for Knoll in 1956–7, were made of reinforced fibreglass moulded into the form of a shell and set on top of a metal pedestal that was designed to look like an extension of the seat. The result looks more like a piece of sculpture than a chair. Indeed, once furniture designers were freed from the tyranny of metal springs and horse-hair stuffings, their creations were restricted only by their imaginations.

Formica became particularly popular. It had been in use in the 1940s, but it was not until the 1950s that it came into its own, replacing virtually all the old enamel-topped tables in kitchens and restaurants. Heat-resistant and hard-wearing, it came in a wide variety of colours and patterns – from abstract designs to simulated wood grain.

The new materials had an impact also on floors and walls. Con-Tact paper (1954), for example, was a glue-backed vinyl film that came in numerous patterns, from marble to trellis work. It was designed to be wiped clean and was easy to hang and easy to peel off, allowing people to change the look of their walls with the minimum of mess and fuss. In Britain the Marley Tile Company produced a range of thermoplastic floor tiles in 19 different colours which were available plain, marbled or monochrome. As with linoleum, the colour pigments went right through the tiles, so that they could not fade or wear out.

For tableware melamine was a favourite material. It was ideally suited as it was unbreakable, and it came in a wide range of rich colours. Melamine was in fact more expensive than china; nevertheless, by the end of the 1950s, about 50 per cent of all dinnerware sold in shops was made from it, and famous industrial designers, such as Raymond Loewy, were fashioning sets.

Here is a lovely Marley Tile Floor which you can lay yourself, or, if you wish, we will lay it for you. See MARLEY HOMELAY floor tiles in your local store, furnishers or builders' merchant, or write for details to MARLEY, Dept. 22, Sevenoaks, Kent.

Floor Tiles by **MARLEY**

SHE SEES... taste-tempting family "treats," cooked to perfection in her all new Wear-Ever... the bright, new aluminum utensils now with c-o-o-l Bakelite® handles and satin-smooth, easy-to-clean interiors... utensils that spread heat evenly to pamper food flavors.

SHE SEES... coffee that wins his brightest, fondest smile... fresh-brewed by today's surest, most advanced coffee maker. By Wear-Ever Aluminum, of course! And best of all, available now at greatly reduced prices in 2, 4, 6, 8 and 12-cup sizes, for a limited time only.

Standard of Quality for over 50 years

wear-ever **aluminum**

Wear-Ever Aluminum, Inc., New Kensington, Pa.

Inside the New Home

The 1950s saw the emergence of the designer from the backroom. In the United States, in particular, names such as Charles and Ray Eames, Raymond Loewy, Florence Knoll and Eero Saarinen became famous to many consumers.

The modern movement in art and design had been advanced rather than crushed by World War II, for the rise of the Nazis drove many leading designers – such as those from the Bauhaus – out of Germany to countries such as the United States, which were anxious to support anything the Nazis had rejected. In the 1950s the Museum of Modern Art, New York, and the Design Centre, London (opened 1956), were keen to promote new design. They consequently ran series of exhibitions intended to introduce the latest ideas to the general public.

The overall look aimed for by designers of interiors and furniture was smooth and streamlined. In a kitchen, for example, ovens and cupboards would be built-in and everything would be made to coordinate – the work surfaces with the table-top and the cooker with the refrigerator. The kitchen was also made more comfortable and more of a family room. In fact, distinctions between the 'correct' use of different rooms began to blur. The whole concept of rooms being used for one activity only – just for dining or just for playing – was going out of favour. Designers were moving toward more open-plan interiors, with 'areas' rather than rooms. These large spaces were broken up by tall bookshelves, part walls or movable partitions.

Colours, patterns and different materials – such as stone and wood – were important means of defining space. Magazines and decorators advocated experimentation with these. For example, Roger Smithells wrote in the *Daily Mail's Ideal Home Book* (1951): 'Several patterns can lie down together like the ideal lamb with the ideal lion without one eating up the other.' Furnishing companies such as Sanderson went so far as to produce ranges of fabrics and wallpapers that contrasted 'harmonically'. The patterns favoured for fabrics and wallpaper tended to be flat and geometric, drawing inspiration from artists such

■ Two extremes of design, as shown by Harry Bertoia's 'Wire' chair (**above**) and Charles Eames's comfortable lounge chair (**far right**).

■ **Right** The most popular interior design look of the 1950s was smooth and streamlined, with built-in coordinating kitchens becoming everyone's ideal.

as Joan Miró and Paul Klee. Primitive motifs, such as images of African warriors, were also popular, as were abstract shapes – for example, the boomerang or the palette.

As far as furniture went, designers turned their backs on the bulky, sensible, rounded, austerity-style look of the 1940s and produced sculptural, often asymmetrical, pieces in unexpected materials and colours. They aimed for simplicity, sleek lines and distinctive shapes. Of the classic chairs, Knoll's Hardoy or 'Butterfly', Harry Bertoia's 'Wire', Eero Saarinen's 'Womb' and George Nelson's 'Coconut' stand out as examples of this approach. Although quite different in their look, these pieces shared one characteristic – they all had the thin, tubular steel legs which became so very popular in the 1950s.

It would be a mistake to think that furniture manufacturers were producing only 'Modern' or 'Contemporary' pieces at this time. In fact, many people wanted reproductions of antiques as well as rustic styles, and were not inhibited about mixing them with the more daring new designs. It was not uncommon for a house to have a modern streamlined kitchen and an 'early American' or Regency-style living room. And, while the more solid look of traditional furniture did not in truth mix well with the lighter-weight modern designs, it was as an acceptable combination to the mass of the population as that of new materials such as Formica with old materials such as wood and stone.

■ **Right** Fabric designers of the 1950s often produced patterns influenced by primitive art or, as here, the Italian Commedia dell'Arte.

25

Products by Design

Only after World War II was the importance of product design and the industrial designer fully realized, with manufacturers discovering that it took more to sell an item than simply that it worked.

After the war there arose a desire to educate the public about 'good design', and all over the world associations sprang up to advance this cause. In Britain the Council of Industrial Designers founded the Design Centre in 1956, in Italy there was the Associazione per Il Disegno Industriale (formed 1956), in France the Institut de l'Esthétique Industrielle (1950), in Germany Rat für Formeburg (1951), and in Japan the Japanese Industrial Designers' Association (1952). These organizations sponsored exhibitions and gave prizes for good design, sometimes in association with museums, galleries or shops. For example, in Italy La Rinascente, a department store, staged shows and awarded the Compasso d'Oro for good design.

It was Europe rather than the United States that took the lead in product design – most US designers were concentrating more on automobile, furniture and interior design. Italy led the field, particularly in electrical goods, with designers such as Ettore Sottsass Jr, Gino Sarfatti and the Castiglioni brothers, Achille and Periacomo, who were responsible for the 'Turbino' light for Flos (1950). Italian styling was very simple, with pure lines and no extraneous detail. Companies such as Arteluce and Olivetti adopted a minimal approach which swiftly won them international acclaim. In the eyes of the world, the name Olivetti came to epitomize modern Italian style; in 1952 the company was honoured by an exhibition in New York's Museum of Modern Art. The company's main designer, Marcello Nizzoli, produced goods as diverse as the Lettera 22 portable typewriter in 1950 and the Divisumma 24 calculator in 1956, but all bore the unmistakeable stamp of the Olivetti style.

German products, too, had a distinctive style – due in no small part to the design college Hochschule für Gestaltung, founded in 1955. This school was originally intended to revive Bauhaus ideals, but its curriculum soon became broader. It established very strong links with industry, particularly with Braun, which used three designers associated with the college – Dieter Rams, Otl Aicher and Hans Gugelot. They aimed for a very simple geometrical style, with harmony of parts as their ultimate goal. Braun had a 'machine aesthetic' and its products, such as the Model 550 shaver, seemed to be exercises in pure form.

Elsewhere in Europe, Britain and Scandinavia were likewise breaking ground in product design

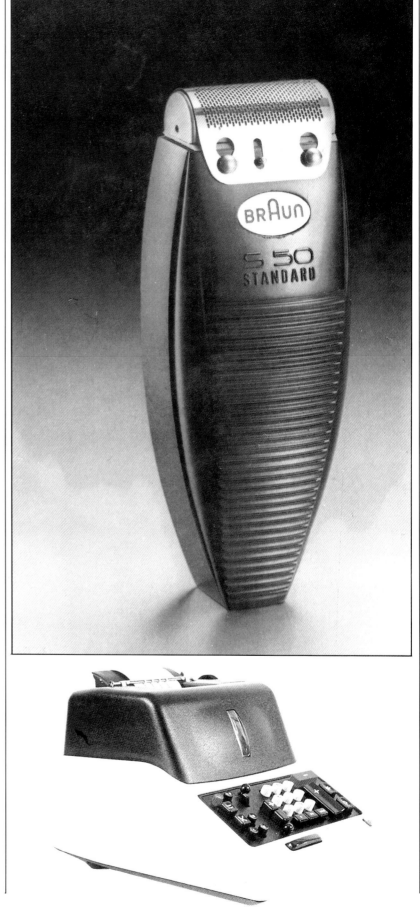

■ **Opposite above** Braun's model 550 shaver: a classic which seems to be an exercise in pure form.

■ **Opposite below** Olivetti's Divisumma 24 calculator, designed by Marcello Nizzoli, bore the unmistakable stamp of the company's stylish simplicity.

■ **Above** The Sony TR-55 transistor radio helped Japan win a share of the vast US market and proved that styling did help sell goods.

■ **Right** Designers came out of the backroom in the 1950s, and companies realized that even relatively straightforward items such as irons needed that extra something to help them sell.

Time has swept away many of the things that did so much to waste it — many that are now remindful of hours grudgingly and drudgingly spent

THE modern way of life has demanded and developed the means of living it. Among the striking examples of progress, there is none more outstanding, in the domestic scene, than the Morphy-Richards Safety Electric Iron — famous all over the world as 'the iron with the tell-tale light.' Here indeed is true design for efficiency and for ease.

MORPHY-RICHARDS LTD · 121 VICTORIA STREET · LONDON, S.W.1

— Scandinavian companies such as Saab and Electrolux were exploring new paths and Britain had successfully combined popular and good taste in the 'Festival Style'. Outside Europe, Japan was forging ahead with reconstruction. This country was strongly influenced by the United States due to its occupation (until 1952), and throughout the 1950s Japanese manufacturers and designers visited the United States to find out about design techniques, products and management. Production methods took precedence over design at the beginning of the decade but, as soon as these had become fast and efficient, manufac-turers turned their attentions to design. Companies such as Toshiba and Sharp set up design departments. Sony, known as TTK (Tokyo Tsushin Kogyo) at the start of the decade, did not set up a design unit until the early 1960s, but from 1954 it had had its own designer; their influence can be seen in goods ranging from the TR–55 transistor radio (1955) to the TV-8-301 portable miniature television (1959). Once Japan realized that styling helped sell goods, nothing could stop its trading expansion and soon it was ready to take on the West – and, in particular, its former mentor, the United States.

Enter the Space Age

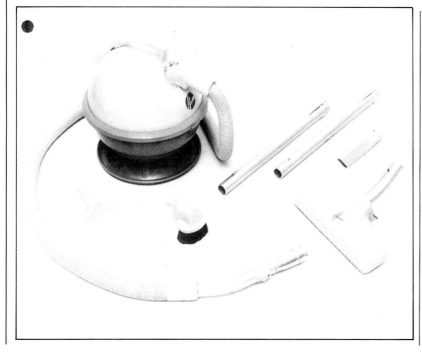

■ **Above** What started as a child's preoccupation quickly became an adult obsession when the first Sputnik was launched in 1957 and the space race got under way.

■ **Left** Space technology had a huge impact on product design, as this satellite-shaped Hoover Constellation vacuum cleaner shows.

■ From pencil boxes, **left,** to chocolate boxes, **below,** rocket ships and spacemen abounded. That final frontier had been conquered and now anything was possible.

The Return to *Haute Couture*

During any war one of the first consumer industries to suffer is the textiles industry – labour is in short supply, imports of raw goods drop, and whatever material is produced is promptly snatched up by the military. World War II was no exception, and its shortages shaped the fashion of the time.

In 1947, however, all the wartime 'make do and mend' measures were thrown aside. The return of extravagance and style was heralded by the unveiling in Paris of Christian Dior's 'New Look'. This flouted all the post-war conventions of austerity by creating a fuller silhouette which needed yards of (still scarce) material. The return to luxury symbolized by this look was particularly apparent in evening wear, in which such opulent fabrics as satins and silks abounded, with fur being the most popular trim.

The style caused uproar throughout Western Europe and the United States. In France women wearing 'New Look' dresses risked having them torn from their backs, while in the United States and Britain people took to the streets *en masse* to protest at the waste of material. Yet, despite the furore, by 1948–9 the style was firmly entrenched and had been generally accepted. It was a look that was to shape *haute couture* throughout the early part of the 1950s. After the drab 1940s women wanted glamour, and designers such as Jacques Fath from France, Balenciaga from Spain and Charles James from the United States set out to give it to them.

Evening dresses in the early 1950s tended to be strapless, with tight-boned bodices and full, sweeping bouffant skirts held in shape by stiffened petticoats. The emphasis, as in Dior's 'New Look', was on the waist, and the most popular silhouette was the 'hourglass' shape. For day wear there were two main silhouettes – the straight and slender for dresses and suits (which many women achieved only with the aid of a corset), and the wide, ample look used for coats. Sometimes these full cape-like coats were abandoned in favour of broad fabric stoles.

Collars were an important design feature. They ranged in style from small, rolled or Chinese-influenced to the large, matelot-shaped or stand-up look. Schiaparelli, for example, specialized in huge jut-out collars that hid the chin.

Accessories such as gloves and hats were vital – more so, in many ways, than shoes, the styling of which had moved away from the platform soles and peep toes of the 1940s toward needle-thin stiletto heels, created by the Italians. Certainly no outfit (day or evening) was complete without gloves. In the evening these were long, made of satin or chamois and coloured to complement the dress. In the day they were shorter, simpler and more often made of plain leather. Hats ranged in style from wide-brimmed, feather-trimmed part-veiled creations to small pert pillboxes or domes. Some designers, such as Dior, took hats so seriously that they became an integral part of their collections.

Even so, hats were already beginning to become less popular. The hat's decline in favour was caused mainly by advances in hair products and styling. Although short hair was still very fashionable, the longer locks of such Hollywood stars as Marilyn Monroe and Lana Turner persuaded many women to let their hair grow. The flood of new hair-tints and shampoos – and, above all, the arrival of rollers and lacquers – ensured that hair dressing became a boom industry. For the hat, the writing was on the wall.

■ **Top** Charles James took the US fashion world by storm with his sweeping, bouffant skirts with their elegant bustles – all made in the finest satins and chiffon. His wife modelled this creation in Chicago in 1955.

■ **Right** The master at work: Christian Dior chooses fabric in his studio.

■ **Above** Dior's 'new look', a style needing an abundance of material, which in the austerity of Europe and the United States after the war caused an uproar but which nevertheless transformed high fashion.

Quality for the Masses

The rise of mass production in the early 1950s had a profound effect on the clothing industry. Before World War II ready-to-wear clothes had been shoddy, humdrum and badly made, but new methods of production brought an end to all that. British companies such as Marks & Spencer could make good-quality clothes that incorporated fashion details, such as collars and cuffs, borrowed from the Parisian *haute couture* collections to give their clothes a touch of 'class'.

The United States, too, was coming into its own at this time. Buyers from the large department stores still went to Paris or Rome for models to copy, and magazines such as *Vogue* and *Harper's Bazaar*, which had a huge influence on fashion in Britain, the United States and France, were still reporting European ideas. However, they were beginning to take note of the homegrown product. This, the 'American Look' in all its variations, was picked up in Europe, where people were exposed to it through the cinema and imported US magazines.

For women the look could be broken down into five main sections: Mexican-influenced, Canadian-influenced, College and Bobby Soxers, Tomboys, and Sweater Girls. The popularity of the last of these styles shows the power of the cinema, as it was made popular primarily by stars such as Lana Turner, Jane Russell and Marilyn Monroe. Besides the most obvious physical attributes, the look relied upon the new cantilevered, pointed bra created by Howard Hughes, and it was eagerly seized upon by European women – indeed, in France the new bras were advertised with the slogan 'Le véritable busty-look Americain'!

In sharp contrast to this very adult image, the College and Bobby Soxers style involved a rather little-girl look, with circular, ballerina-length cancan skirts puffed out with petticoats and often appliquéd with a popular motif, such as a French scene or a pattern of poodles. Culottes, too, were popular, and were worn with the ubiquitous Bobby Sox, pumps or plimsolls. Rare recognition of this youthful style as an element of fashion came in 1952, when *Vogue* ran a feature about 17–25-year-olds entitled 'Young Idea'. It was not long before retailers, particularly in the United States, realized there was a lucrative market to be tapped.

Separates were becoming very important, with designers such as Bonnie Cashin in the United States creating a 'layered look' that was practical as well as stylish. For women who did not feel that the College look, the frilly Mexican-style dresses or 'shirtwaisters' suited them, there were always stretch ski pants, the three-quarter length Pedal Pushers and Capri Pants or, for the really

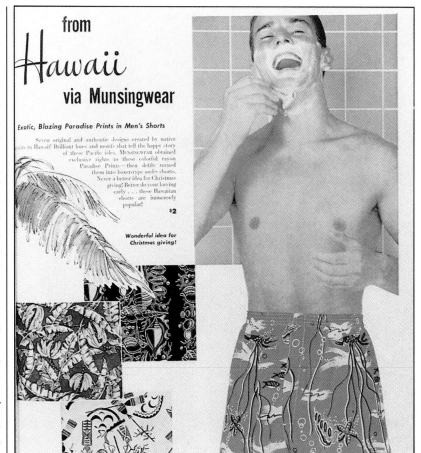

from **Hawaii** via Munsingwear

Exotic, Blazing Paradise Prints in Men's Shorts

Seven original and authentic designs created by native artists in Hawaii! Brilliant hues and motifs that tell the happy story of these Pacific isles. Munsingwear obtained exclusive rights to these colorful rayon Paradise Prints—then deftly turned them into boxer-type under-shorts. Never a better idea for Christmas giving! Better do your buying early . . . these Hawaiian shorts are immensely popular!

$2

Wonderful idea for Christmas giving!

adventurous, miners' denim Levis – first worn as women's fashion items in California.

As far as men were concerned, *haute couture* ignored them: most clothes were still very conservative. Nevertheless, casual fashion was taking off. The pre-war grey flannel trousers and navy blue serge soon gave way to sports jackets and slacks. Men were still expected to wear the corporate businessman's uniform of the dull, dark suit for work, but in their leisure time they had far more freedom.

There were various popular styles: the soft look of the European city businessman, wearing a light lounge suit and slip-on shoes; the hard look favoured by younger men, consisting of a heavy jacket worn over slim trousers, ideally Levis; and the casual sporting look. This last style, which started on US college campuses, stressed comfort and was very lightweight. Men would wear flannel trousers, button-down shirts and thin ties; the more flamboyant of them donned reversible waistcoats and sports jackets of fancy tweed – sometimes threaded with Lurex. And for those barbecues and trips to the coast there were Bermuda (and later Jamaica) shorts, T-shirts and the Hawaiian shirt.

Leisure dressing had arrived.

■ **Above, above right, below right** Leisure dressing for men and women: the US ideal of the outdoor life getting the designers' stamp of approval. At last it had become permissible for men as well as women to wear bright colours.

■ **Far right** Three-quarter-length pedalpushers and tight jumpers were an ideal way of achieving 'Le véritable busty-look Americain'!

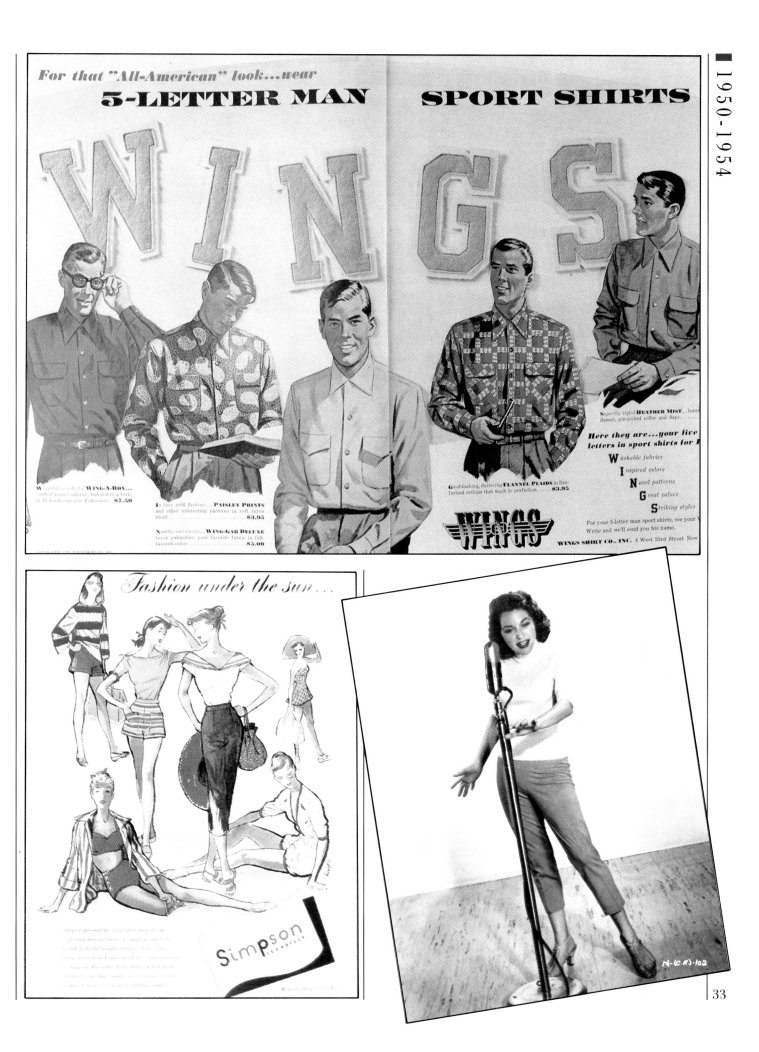

N-(C-R)-102

Ideal Home

One of the biggest problems governments faced after World War II was providing enough housing. In Britain and the rest of Europe the bombs had destroyed numerous buildings – indeed whole areas – and this seemed the ideal opportunity to start from scratch and build something better. Each country approached the task differently. Britain took elements of the US building programme and adapted them to its own needs. While the United States was building vast tracts of suburban dwellings such as Levittown, Long Island, the British decided to build whole new towns outside the old urban centres – particularly London. These new towns would, it was hoped, relieve the cities' congestion and provide decent cheap housing for the overspill population. For example, Basildon, Stevenage and Harlow were built around London. By the end of the 1950s one out of every five families had moved into a new home.

At this time Britain also built its first high-rise blocks. Although these were acclaimed architecturally, they did not prove popular with their inhabitants. Other European countries, such as France and Italy, likewise built large apartment blocks, many of which, such as Le Corbusier's Unité d'Habitation at Marseilles (1947–52), were more successful than their British counterparts.

The ideal home of the 1950s had a modern uncluttered look. It might be split-level with glass walls, such as Mies van der Rohe's US houses of that time, but for those desiring more conventional houses the right look could be achieved by getting rid of interior walls and opting for an open-plan layout.

The kitchen – the heart of the house – was a vital part of the ideal home. Here it was that the push-button age entered its forte. These buttons did not really represent any new technological breakthroughs, but they were symbolic of a utopian future – a brave new world where household drudgery would cease to exist. Magazines predicted futuristic houses where a push of a button would be enough to activate the washing machine, the automatic floor sweeper, the automatic window cleaner and the robotic duster. Numerous articles appeared about the home of the future, often described as being in the 1980s, where even things such as wall colours could be changed by the push of a button. To a reasonable extent, of course, these predictions have been borne out, as have other 'marvels' beyond the imaginations of the 1950s prophets.

In the 1950s kitchen, washing machines, food blenders and even cookers were operated by buttons. As these labour-saving devices proliferated, people found themselves with more leisure time.

According to the ideal-home mentality, this time should have been spent with the family, either out of doors pursuing sporty activities or clustered around the television set. Yet the reality of 1950s home life was not always so ideal, and not every family could attain a place in the affluent society. In Britain, for example, more than 3 million families were still living in slums by the end of the decade, and in the United States, while middle-class whites were moving out of the cities into the new suburbs, the poor black populations were left behind, forgotten and neglected, in overcrowded tenements.

To cap it all, even the nuclear family, regarded as so important in the 1950s, was beginning to disintegrate: divorce rates were rising steadily, young adults were leaving home at an earlier age and children were beginning to question their parents' values.

■ Harlow New Town, outside London (**right**), and Le Corbusier's Unité d'Habitation at Marseilles (**below**): two approaches to solving the post-war housing crisis.

Butlin's THE IDEAL FAMILY HOLIDAY

FREE BROCHURE: Send postcard to:—
BUTLIN'S LTD., (Dept. H.B.) 439 OXFORD STREET, LONDON, W.1

Lucky me!

■ **Left** Happy families: shorter working hours and automation led to an increase in leisure time in the 1950s.

■ **Above** The push-button age: labour-saving devices such as washing machines brought a welcome release from drudgery for many housewives.

35

■ Left and bottom No home was complete without one: television was the most popular way of relaxing in the 1950s. In the United States alone the number of people owning sets rose by 47 million over the decade. One of the most familiar faces on the box was the irrepressible Lucille Ball in *I Love Lucy*.

■ Right Televisions came in all shapes and sizes, but few were as strange-looking as this 1959 Braun set.

■ Below The coronation of Queen Elizabeth II in 1953 gave television in the UK an incredible boost.

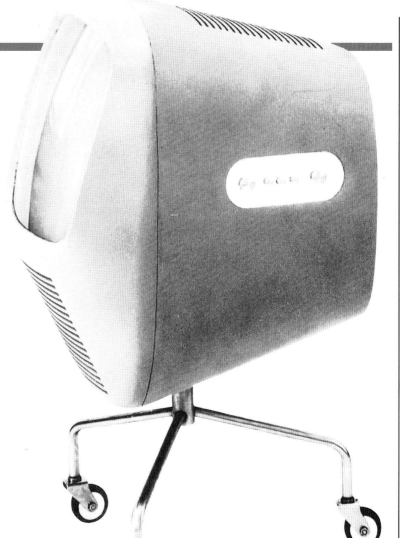

The interior of the Guggenheim Museum, New York, designed by Frank Lloyd Wright and completed in 1959.

1955-1959

'You've never had it so good'

In the West the second half of the 1950s was characterized by growing prosperity and increased spending power. Harold MacMillan, Britain's Conservative Prime Minister, said to his country in 1959: 'You've never had it so good.' The affluent consumer society had arrived.

In Europe the car, television and fridge became the essential status symbols, while average people in the United States, who had possessed such items for many years, now wanted them to be bigger and 'better' to fulfil their idea of the American Dream. Cars were huge, finned monsters which guzzled the cheap fuel; televisions were set in large, wooden cabinets; and kitchens had to be models of streamlined, automated efficiency. The increased use of technology and automation at home and in factories meant that people had more leisure time. The advent of the transatlantic telephone service in 1956 and the appearance of the first transatlantic US commercial aircraft in 1958 meant that communications between the Old World and the New were greatly strengthened.

In Europe, meanwhile, Italy, West Germany and France were setting out on the road to Rome by establishing the European Union in 1955. This agreement led to the signing of the Treaty of Rome in 1957 and so to the creation of the European Economic Community or, as it became popularly known, the Common Market.

It was a time of forgiveness and reconciliation as far as the Allies and the Axis were concerned. The wounds caused by World War II were beginning to heal. In 1955 West Germany was allowed to join NATO (established by the North Atlantic Treaty in 1949), and a year later Japan, by now a thriving economic force, was admitted to the United Nations. Nevertheless, although people were enjoying unparalleled standards of living, political crises still loomed large. Moreover, there was the spectre of racial tension that was so to dog the 1960s. This unrest became very apparent in the United States in 1955 when Martin Luther King, a black Baptist minister from Montgomery, Alabama, founded an association to abolish segregated seating on local buses – a goal achieved in 1956. The other big racial battle in the United States was related: segregation in schools. The first major clashes took place in Little Rock, Arkansas, in 1957 and 1958, when the National Guard was sent in to keep the peace and enforce integration, although this was not to be fully attained until 1960. In Britain, meanwhile, racial unrest and prejudice erupted in 1958 in the form of race riots in the Notting Hill Gate region of London.

As far as world politics were concerned, the

LITTLE ROCK CENT

■ **Above** Little Rock High School, Arkansas, 1957: the US government showed its determination to end segregation in schools by sending in armed troops to escort nine black students to classes.

■ **Left** The Soviet invasion of Hungary in 1956 showed how impotent the West was against the might of Russia.

■ **Below** Fidel Castro's overthrow of the Cuban dictator Fulgencio Batista in 1959 signalled a period of East–West confrontation which was to peak in the early 1960s.

late 1950s saw no lessening of the East/West tension.

In 1956 Soviet troops intent on quelling an uprising invaded Hungary. The West was unwilling to get involved, so stood aside impotently as the Soviet Union proved its domination over Eastern Europe. In 1957 the war of words spread to space, with the launch of the USSR's Sputnik 1, the first artificial satellite. And the USSR was looking westward, too – to Cuba, right on the United States' doorstep. In 1959 Fidel Castro overthrew the dictator Fulgencio Batista and established a new regime which aligned itself with the Soviet Bloc and denounced the United States, which had supported Batista. More important, Castro's government began to seize US property – $1 billion's worth by the end of the decade. Confrontation seemed inevitable and caused worldwide concern.

In the Middle East, France and Britain were likewise caught up in a confrontation. This took place in 1956 and was over the Suez Canal – a vital trade route to the east – which had been seized by the new Egyptian president, Abdul Gamal Nasser. The two countries landed troops in Egypt but soon found that international opinion was against them: they were forced to make an ignominious withdrawal.

What might have seemed a minor issue at the time was that Western society itself faced rebellion from within. By the late 1950s teenagers had become a force to be reckoned with. They had a great deal of leisure time and they had money. They were looking for a style radically different from that of their parents.

All over the Western world, these teenagers represented a vast market that was just waiting to be exploited.

The Teenager is Born

The term 'teenager' did not come into general use until the mid-1950s. Until that time there was no recognized middle ground between childhood and adulthood – indeed, once children left school (in most Western countries at the age of 14) and started their first job, they were popularly, although not legally, considered as adults. For many this change took place overnight: it was only in the most privileged of families that young people were allowed a period of grace between their childhood and 'coming out'.

The main change that took place in the 1950s and which led to the recognition of teenagers as a separate entity was the growth of the affluent society. Young people were earning good wages; even if they were still at school, they could take a part-time or a Saturday job. As they had none of the responsibilities of adults, no families to support, they could spend nearly all their earnings on themselves. The advent of the five-day week and generally shorter working hours gave them plenty of leisure time in which to spend that money. Teenagers suddenly became important consumers – a fact that did not long escape the attention of manufacturers and retailers – and young people soon developed very strong ideas about what they wanted to spend their money on.

Teenagers were likewise firm about how they wanted to use their leisure time. They wanted their own places to go to, away from adults and adult authority. Numerous milk and coffee bars, dance halls and jazz clubs sprang up where teenagers could congregate. Youth clubs, too, became popular, and in many countries were supported by governments who felt that it was important to give teenagers a place where they could be entertained and kept off the streets and out of trouble. In Britain youth clubs were especially favoured, particularly among 14–18-year-olds; in fact, in the early 1950s about four out of every ten young people in this age group belonged to a club, and the ratio increased throughout the decade.

Along with the growth of affluence and independence among the young came an increase in assertiveness and the seeds of rebellion. Teenagers began to reject the values of their parents and react against their lifestyles. They chose as their heroes actors such as James Dean and Marlon Brando who played alienated, disaffected youths in films such as *Rebel Without a Cause* (1955) and *On the Waterfront* (1954).

Teenage dissatisfaction took more active form in the shape of law-breaking. Juvenile delinquency became a problem in the United States and all the Western European countries to the extent that in England, for example, the number of crimes committed by people aged under 21

almost doubled in the years between 1955 and 1959. Vandalism became commonplace, and teenagers on both sides of the Atlantic formed themselves into gangs – a subject dwelt upon by numerous movies. Many of the gangs or groups adopted very distinctive styles of dress; these, like uniforms, gave them a corporate identity and made them stand out. In Britain the Teddy Boys (known colloquially as 'teds') were the most prevalent of these youth groups. This movement, which started among the working class in south London in 1954–5, soon spread throughout the country and gradually, in the eyes of many adults, became synonymous with violence – particularly as the Teddy Boys played a very prominent role in the 1958 race riots in London's Notting Hill Gate. Teddy Boys wore clothes that parodied those of the Edwardian era: tight straight 'drainpipe' trousers and long 'drape' jackets, often with velvet collars and cuffs.

While Teddy Boys remained a very British movement through the 1950s, other groups, such as the Beatniks, attracted a much more international following. Yet the vast majority of teenagers showed their rebellion merely by wearing as their customary dress jeans and a T-shirt – clothes which, because of their association with manual labour, symbolized a breaking away from and rejection of every aspiration their parents had for them.

■ **Right** The British Teddy Boys wore clothes which parodied those of the Edwardian era, but there was nothing old-fashioned about their behaviour.

■ **Far right** The potential spending power of teenagers made them important consumers, and service industries exemplified by this hairdressing salon, sprang up in the 1950s to cater exclusively to them.

■ James Dean (**below**) and Marlon Brando (**opposite, main picture**) acted out on the cinema screen what many teenagers were feeling in real life – alienation and disaffection.

■ **Bottom** Every teenager's dream, a room of his or her own – here complete with pin-up and Chianti bottle.

Rock'n'Roll

Youth came into its own in the 1950s. The teens, particularly, were seen as exciting years, and by the middle of the decade there appeared a type of music that seemed to encapsulate and reflect everything a teenager felt – excitement, love and rebellion. This music was rock'n'roll, and it was to take the world by storm.

The term 'rock' was not new – it had first been used in a musical context in the 1920s – and in 1935 Joe Haymes had brought out a record called 'Rock and Roll' ('roll' being, like 'jazz', a negro term for sex). Rock'n'roll had its origins in the southern United States. It was a combination of black music – primarily 12-bar blues – with poor-white Country and Western music derived from rural US hillbilly music. The strong, repetitive rhythms of the blues interacted potently with C&W's more extrovert approach to produce a form of music called 'rockabilly' (a term nowadays used to describe hillbilly music with a strong rock element). From rockabilly and the independently developed rhythm'n'blues (R&B) sprang rock'n'roll.

One of the early proponents of rockabilly, Carl Perkins, managed to sell one million copies of his 'Blue Suede Shoes' record (1956). The real breakthrough for rock'n'roll had, however, come a year earlier with the release of 'Rock Around the Clock' by Bill Haley and the Comets, a song from the soundtrack of the 1955 teen-rebel film *The Blackboard Jungle*; after the success of the record, Haley went on to make a film of the same name. Produced on a small budget – $200,000 – this film introduced rock'n'roll to a wider international audience and proved a great success. It made $1 million in its first year and roused teenagers all over the world to dance in the aisles of the cinemas where it was shown – something never seen before. It was also blamed for juvenile delinquency; for example, when it was shown in London in 1956, 2,000 young people rioted in the Elephant and Castle area 'incited by the film'.

The reaction to the movie *Rock Around the Clock* convinced many adults that rock'n'roll, with its wild rhythms and sexual undertones, was a bad influence on the young. In Britain the BBC refused for many years to acknowledge its existence: as US radio stations, with their constant airplay, fuelled the market for rock'n'roll, British radio simply ignored it. In fact it was not until the late 1950s that the BBC accepted the new music and that television programmes such as the BBC's *Juke Box Jury* and ITV's *Six-Five Special* began to recognize rock'n'roll's existence.

The early rock'n'roll musicians were often black – for example, Chuck Berry and Little Richard – and hence did not receive the coverage they merited, so it was not until the arrival of a young white Memphis truck driver that a 'star' was born. That truck driver was Elvis Presley and he, more than any other performer, turned rock'n' roll into a high-profile international form of music for the young and a big earner for the record companies. His first single, 'That's All Right Mama', was released in 1954. In 1956 he held the number-one slot in the US hit parade continuously from August to December.

Elvis became the figurehead of a new culture, which had its own clothes, language (jive talk), dance (jitterbugging) and subgroups (such as the Teddy Boys in Britain). His famous sneer and provocative pelvic movements filled parents everywhere with the dread that their children would be corrupted – to the extent that, when he appeared on the famous *Ed Sullivan Show* on US television, he was allowed to be shown only from the waist up! What parents failed to realize was that their disapproval of rock'n'roll merely added to its attractiveness as far as the young were concerned. Soon singers were appearing with pseudonyms that reflected everything parents most feared – Marty Wilde, Billy Fury and Vince Eager.

■ **Above** Bill Haley and the Comets introduced rock'n'roll to the world in the film *Rock Around the Clock* (1956), which roused teenagers to dance in the aisles of the cinemas where it was shown.

■ **Above right** Manufacturers, anxious to cash in on rock'n'roll's popularity, thought up more and more ideas for novelties.

■ **Right** In the late 1950s even the then-staid BBC finally recognized the existence of the new music with its *Six-Five Special*.

■ **Below right** Elvis: the first rock'n'roll star and a bad boy who wowed the young and worried their parents with his sneer and pelvic thrusts.

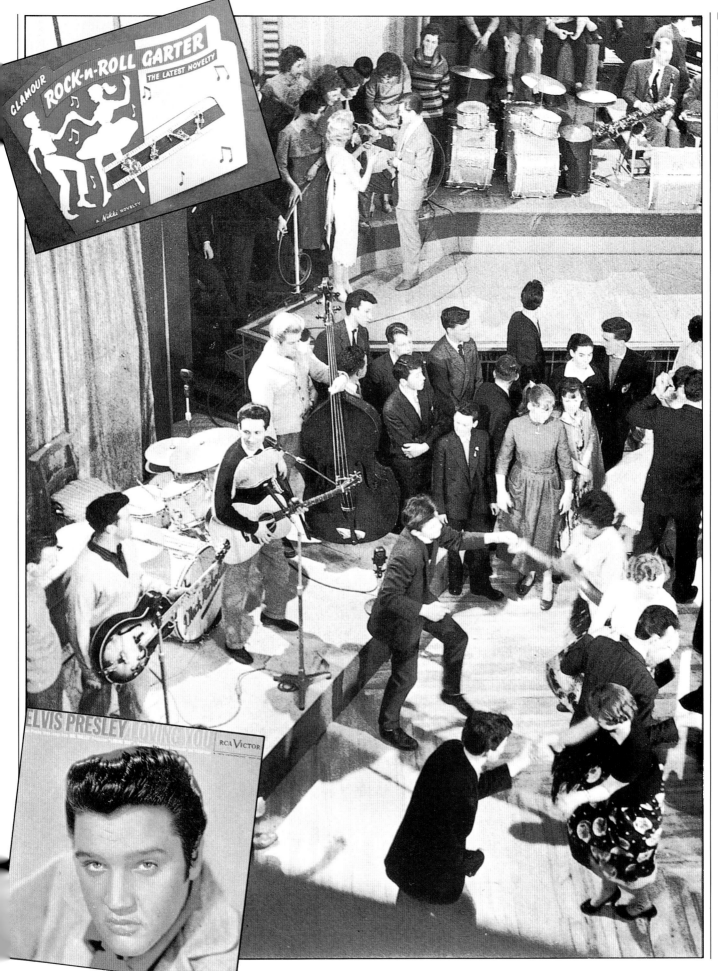

The Tarnished Silver Screen

Mainstream cinema in the 1950s was in a state of flux. After its post-war success – in both the United States and Britain highest-ever audience figures were recorded in 1946 – attendance started to drop. Hollywood, riven with paranoia because of the McCarthyite witch-hunts, found that its tried and tested recipes for success, teaming stars together or producing series of movies, could no longer be relied upon to pull in the public. For people in the United States had discovered the joys of television. Moreover, many had moved to the suburbs, miles from any cinema, where they were enjoying an affluent lifestyle: they no longer required the escapism provided by the movies.

The success of mainstream films seemed to be a matter of pot luck, so Hollywood dabbled in genre movies – Westerns such as *Shane* (1953), musicals such as *Singin' in the Rain* (1952), science-fiction movies like *Invasion of the Body Snatchers* (1956) and even social-comment films such as *On the Waterfront* (1954) – in an attempt to find a winning formula. In desperation, film makers even resorted to using such gimmicks as 3-D and Cinerama to attract audiences.

In Britain it took a little longer for the affluent society to arrive, and so in the early 1950s the film industry could still rely upon an audience wanting relief from the shabbiness of everyday life. Yet the film makers were lacking in direction and innovation, and in the first half of the decade relied on producing films about the recent war, such as *The Cruel Sea* (1953) and *The Dam Busters* (1955), as well as on comedies. These latter were mainly made at the Ealing Studios – indeed, so many were made there that the name became synonymous with British cinematic humour. But these comedies, with their concentration on eccentric British characters and institutions, were unfathomable to any foreign audience and so could never become commercial blockbusters. After *The Ladykillers* (1955), the Ealing Studios were sold to the BBC, and the company went downhill until its demise in 1959. Ironically, many of the Ealing comedies are now held in high regard all over the world.

While the British and US film industries were declining the French and, particularly, the Italians were going from strength to strength. The French cinema was commercially the healthiest in Europe during the 1950s – there was a great deal of production and the industry had full government support and, importantly, intellectual respectability. However, although a great many films were made, they were often undistinguished and, until the end of the decade and the arrival of

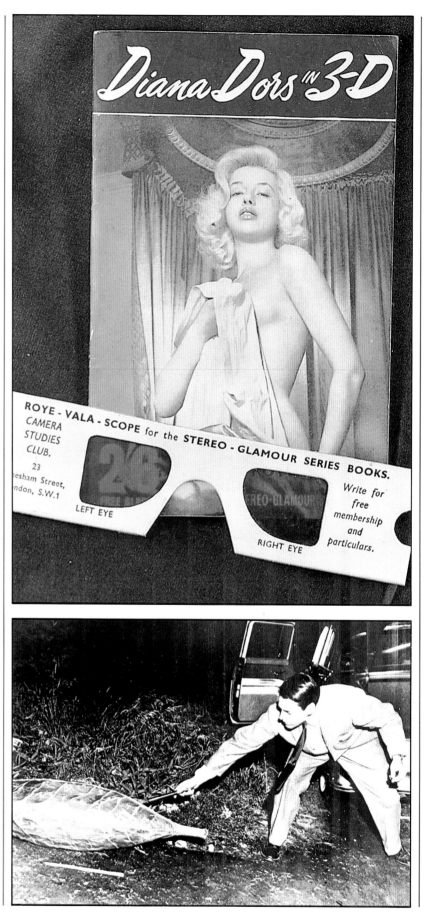

the 'Nouvelle Vague', lacking in any new direction. Moreover, for obvious reasons, distribution was mainly limited to French-speaking territories, so the movies could make only a certain amount of money. French film makers tended to go for Hollywood-influenced thrillers, period pieces and sex comedies.

Italian cinema was in the midst of its most exciting and productive time, with film makers such as Rosselini, Visconti and Fellini suddenly getting worldwide acknowledgement. At the start of the decade Italian directors had been making neo-realist movies that dealt with the country's poor, but this movement basically came to an end around 1951–2, when different types of films, notably more frivolous ones, began to be made, many in coproduction with US companies. Before the 1950s Italian films were often dismissed as 'arty' – maybe for no other reason than that their dialogue was in a language other than English – but now they began to attract large audiences. This was partly because they had a reputation for being racy, partly because stars such as Sophia Loren and Gina Lollobrigida were popular screen goddesses, and partly because of the international hunger at that time for all things Italian. Fellini's *La Dolce Vita* (made in 1959), a movie about the manners and morals of Italian high society, exemplified this changing attitude toward Italian cinema: it was a box-office hit in the United States, aided no doubt by the storm of controversy that surrounded it. The Italian movie of the decade, however, was probably Vittorio De Sica's *Umberto D*, a shattering study of loneliness and old age.

Although the 1950s had started listlessly as far as movies were concerned, by the end of the decade there was a new spirit abroad. Film makers were more prepared to break away from tradition and, more importantly, from the security of the large studios. All over the world film clubs and 'art houses' were opening; these, together with newly inaugurated international film festivals, catered for the developing sophistication of cinema audiences the world around.

■ **Left** *The Seven Samurai,* directed by Akira Kurosawa (1954), was one of the first Japanese films to receive Western recognition due to the inauguration of international film festivals and the desire of the 'art house' audiences to see films other than mainstream Hollywood offerings.

■ **Opposite top left** In their desperation to woo audiences back into the cinema, film-makers resorted to such gimmicks as 3D.

■ In its search for a winning formula, Hollywood dabbled in genre movies ranging from science fiction, such as *Invasion of the Body Snatchers* (**far left**) to musicals such as *Singin' in the Rain* (**above left**).

Angry Young Men

The desire to reject authority and establishment values expressed by many young people during the 1950s was evident also in more academic and intellectual circles. In the United States, while mass-consumerism appeared to have no limits, governments seemed unable to master either internal or external crises. The Korean War dragged on until 1953, drafting people from all social backgrounds as it progressed; hydrogen bombs were being tested; and governments of all persuasions seemed unable to stem the escalating Cold War which threatened to destroy the world. Society, many felt, was sick.

In the United States an 'underground' movement began to emerge. It consisted of writers and intellectuals who preferred to reject society by 'dropping out' altogether. The prophet of this 'beat generation' was the poet Allen Ginsberg, who advocated large doses of peace, drugs, sex and mysticism as the only means of protest. A beat style of dress emerged. It was surprisingly forward-looking, consisting of largely black clothes with glasses and, for men, an obligatory beard. The beatnik style had developed from the look favoured on US college campuses, and reflected the beatniks' rather laid-back, unaggressive approach to life. The standard beat girl might wear black stockings, a short skirt and a duffel-coat, and would sport pale lips and long, loose hair. Around this time an advertisement in the *New Yorker* offered a beat kit, consisting of a beard and a pair of glasses, under the slogan 'Be the First Beatnik on Your Block'.

In Britain, a similar feeling of restlessness and frustration found expression through a group of writers and playwrights popularly dubbed the 'Angry Young Men'. Plays such as John Osborne's *Look Back in Anger* (1956) rejected conventional polite society in favour of a bedsitter environment, and got their anti-establishment message across by means of violence and revolt. By depicting younger and lower-class people on stage, they were influential in breaking down fixed attitudes toward social standards and morality. They also helped promote the belief that everyone had the right to speak and be heard, an idea seminal to the developments of the 1960s.

The growing fashion for challenging the establishment added considerably to the support for the anti-nuclear campaigns which emerged in Germany, Holland and Britain at this time. The British arm of the movement was the Campaign for Nuclear Disarmament (CND), which organized 'Ban the Bomb' marches to Aldermaston (the Atomic Weapons Research Establishment, AWRE) over Easter bank holidays during the late 1950s. While these events were undoubtedly peaceful protests, they did provide people with the opportunity to express their dissatisfaction with the political and social situation. Photographs of the marches were reproduced in the media, and showed young men and women wearing casual, practical clothes, such as duffel-coats, anoraks and rucksacks. As with the beat generation, a particular style of dress came to be an expression of political creeds.

■ **Right** A Beatnik on the steps of the Gaslight Café in New York's Greenwich Village. This venue was the scene of many 'Beat Generation' happenings, including exhibitions and the obligatory poetry readings.

■ **Right** Jack Kerouac's account of life on the back roads of North America in *On the Road* (1955) appealed to the new young and rebellious.

■ **Far right** John Osborne (right) talking to the actor Kenneth Haigh outside the Royal Court Theatre in London. Kenneth Haigh starred in the highly successful production of Osborne's *Look Back in Anger* staged at the Royal Court in 1956.

■ **Below** Anti-nuclear marches to Aldermaston were a regular event on Easter bank holidays during the late 1950s. This march, which followed the Chiswick High Road into London in 1959, included Jacquetta Hawkes and Michael Foot.

Paris and Art

Paris, fresh from throwing off the constraints of the German occupation, sprang to life during the 1950s as a centre for all forms of artistic activity, most notably in the areas of fine art, literature and music. Its association with such romantic literary figures as Jean-Paul Sartre, Simone de Beauvoir and Roland Barthes made the city deeply attractive to any serious-minded man or woman. But the city's appeal was not only cerebral: Gay Paree was open to tourists once more, and they flocked to the city in vast numbers. Many high-class magazines in the United States and Europe, such as *Esquire*, advertised Paris holidays – now available to far more people because of the growth in commercial air travel.

Parisian motifs began to appear everywhere: palettes, streetside cafés, dressed poodles and the Eiffel Tower – all were used on just about every kind of clothing, household fabric and crockery. Designers not only used more popular images, they also looked to the fine artists for inspiration. Many of their chosen artists, such as Joan Miró and Paul Klee, painted free-floating organic abstract images that could be simply translated into repeat fabric or wallpaper designs. Similarly, the abstract shapes of Alexander Calder's mobiles were easily rendered into simple graphic forms. Designers looked to Surrealist artists, particularly Salvador Dali, whose metaphysical images complemented contemporary philosophical ideas. Artists suddenly became gods, and everybody wanted to be one. The art schools of Paris, London and New York breathed with new life.

Several of the major film releases of the period were set in Paris or elsewhere in France, including *An American in Paris* (1951), starring the French Leslie Caron and the American Gene Kelly, and *To Catch a Thief* (1955), starring Grace Kelly and Cary Grant. Leslie Caron – along with Audrey Hepburn – was important in spreading the 'French Look', an impish 'gamine' style of dress that included tight black pedalpushers, flattie shoes, stripey T-shirts, berets, lots of red lipstick and the obligatory Gauloise. The ultimate accessory for the art-student variation of this style was a basket containing a baguette, a bottle of wine, spaghetti and several paint brushes.

Films such as these depicted also the jazz clubs or 'dives' of Paris. Contemporary and traditional jazz came to the fore as the musical emblem of a 'with it' artistic lifestyle, and similar clubs thrived in London's Soho and New York's Greenwich Village. The saxophone motif, which had enjoyed some success in the 1940s, could be found not just on the record sleeve but also on any object or fabric that was willing to accept it.

WITH PERFUME IMPORTED FROM PAR

Don't be angry, Pierre . . . you too will be more admired in the tailored perfection of Eagle Clothes. Throughout the USA, fine men's stores are now exhibiting Eagle's "Holiday for Spring" collection. See the elegant fabrics and fashions . . . the imported Continental weaves of lustered magnificence . . . the triumphs of domestic artistry. Each is an Eagle exclusive – most admired and most desired by the contemporary man. For the name of your nearest dealer, write today to Eagle Clothes, Inc., 1107 Broadway, New York. PREVIEW EAGLE'S "HOLIDAY FOR SPRING" COLLECTION – AND YOU'RE ELIGIBLE TO WIN A PARIS VACATION FOR TWO!

Left Together with Haute Couture fashion, French beauty products were much in demand abroad.

Below left *Paris Holiday*, starring Bob Hope and Anita Ekberg and released in 1957, was just one of a number of major films made during this period that helped to promote France to the rest of the world.

Right *Le Cri* by Joan Miró. Many designers found inspiration in fine art, notably in the haunting abstract images of Miró and Paul Klee.

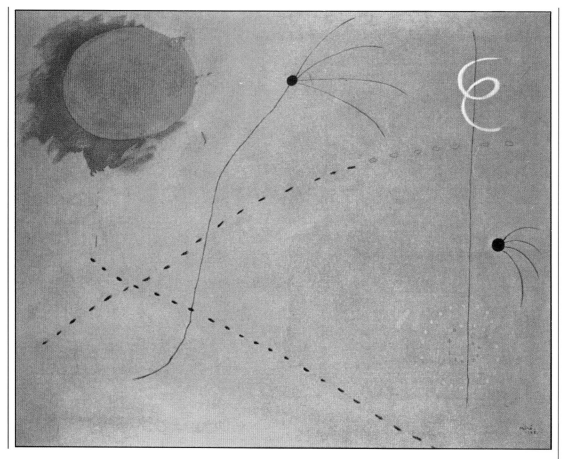

Above An Alfred Meakin saucer from the 1950s. Dressed poodles and other decorative dogs were seen as fundamentally Parisian accessories.

Right Jean-Paul Sartre and Simone de Beauvoir arriving at the Palais de Justice in Paris. To many people, they represented the height of intellectual Parisian society.

Scandinavian Styling

The term 'Scandinavian Modern' is generally used to describe a style of furniture and interior design that first took shape in the 1930s, but reached mass international markets in the late 1940s and 1950s. Although the style undoubtedly owed a debt to both US and Italian sources, it was based on strong Scandinavian design, and used 'natural' materials to create a classically elegant but very contemporary style. Furniture relied heavily on traditional craft principles and was solidly built, ergonomically sound and visually pleasing. Woods such as teak, birch and beech were coupled with leather and glass, although some designers, most notably in Finland, branched out into metals and plastics. Metalwork, glassware and textiles (the other areas in which the Scandinavian countries excelled) were designed with an inherent 'truth to materials' doctrine, and made use of simple yet solid forms.

In time, Scandinavian Modern became debased as more and more manufacturers cashed in on the fashion, but the designs on which the style was founded are examples of simple, comfortable elegance.

Sweden

'Swedish Modern' had already begun to penetrate international markets when Douglas Haskell, the writer, wrote of the 1939 New York World Fair: 'None of the other artistic exhibitions, not even the best, can measure itself in skill with that of the Swedish artists . . . The happy little Swedish pavilion is civilization.' Drawing heavily on pre-war ideals of combining form and function, Swedish furniture manifested pleasing shapes and was designed to be good for your back; above all, however, it was slick and well marketed.

Swedish awareness of the mutual benefits of marrying industry and design is one of the most important factors behind the wholesale acceptance of Scandinavian forms around the world. As an illustration of this, one of the leading Swedish furniture designers of the time, Carl Malmsten, was not only a designer and teacher but also a

■ **Below** Scandinavian promotional stands at Heals, London, in the late 1950s. A major factor behind Scandinavia's success abroad at this time was aggressive marketing.

■ **Above** A bedsitting room designed by Astrid Sampe. As with much Scandinavian interior design of the period, natural woods feature prominently.

■ **Left** Cutlery of the late 1950s, combining the strength of stainless steel and the elegance of polished wood.

■ **Far left** Armchair in bent beechwood with a plaited seat, designed by the Dane Hans Wegner and produced by Fritz Hansen. Wegner trained as a cabinetmaker and was influential in transferring Danish furniture into an international phenomenon.

manufacturer.

Another major area of innovative Swedish design was glassware. Småland, a province in southern Sweden, fostered a large glass-making community, and the Orrefors company produced some striking glassware at this time. Sven Palmquist, a noted designer of the period, experimented with the globular and reflective qualities of glass, whereas Nils Landberg, another highly respected designer, produced elegantly natural blown forms.

Finland

Finnish design of this period was perhaps the boldest and most adventurous to emerge from the Scandinavian countries, and was less tied to the craft tradition. Finnish glass design was particularly exciting, most notably in the work of Tapio Wirkkala and Timo Sarpaneva, manufactured by the Karhula-Iittala company. Both these designers had established careers in other areas of design, but when they applied their talents to glass they produced strikingly unconventional sculptural forms.

Finnish furniture is typified by the pieces manufactured by Asko, using not only wood but also plastic and metal. The bold, abstract designs characteristic of Finnish textiles can be seen in the fabric manufactured by Marimekko. Vuokko Nurmesniemi produced some striking fabric designs for the company, particularly in the 1960s when she was heavily influenced by Pop and Op Art.

Denmark

Danish furniture design, more than that of any other Scandinavian country, looked to the past for inspiration, combining the old patterns with solid, sculptural forms based on modern ergonomic research and aesthetic considerations. Børge Mogensen's 'hunting' chair of 1950 displays both these characteristics. Arne Jacobsen's furniture was more unorthodox, his originality finding expression in later years in his 'egg' and 'swan' chairs that look like the sculptural manifestations of Joan Miró's paintings. Other areas of Danish design that had international appeal were ceramics, glass and, in particular, metalwork. The molten solid forms of Danish metalwork are best seen in Henning Koppel's timeless designs for Georg Jensen and the German firm, Rosenthal.

Building a Modern World

When building picked up again after World War II, the Modern Movement – which had until then been a minority movement, even an embattled one – now became the generally accepted replacement for the traditional styles of architecture. Its apparent simplicity and cheapness appealed to governments committed to rebuilding but whose resources were cripplingly limited, and it had the symbolic appeal of a new architecture for a brave new world. The movement had a high moral tone: the word 'style' was a term of abuse implying triviality and fashion. However, characteristic forms inevitably developed which amounted to a style. Apart from individualists, such as Frank Lloyd Wright and Buckminster Fuller, two main streams are recognizable: first, the pure and puritanical style exemplified by the German Ludwig Mies van der Rohe and, second, the more romantic style exemplified by Le Corbusier (Charles Édouard Jeanneret), a Swiss working in France.

As early as 1919 Mies van der Rohe had designed a model of a skyscraper of glass – that is, one with an internal supporting frame clothed externally on all four sides with a continuous skin of glass (in the architect's own words, a 'skin and bone' architecture). This general form he applied to apartment blocks, office blocks and residential houses, notably the Farnsworth House (1947) in Illinois and the Seagram Building (1958) in New York. The system, with its large areas of glass and consequent depth of light penetration, has become a standard worldwide, particularly for office blocks.

The distinction of Mies van der Rohe's own buildings is their perfection and precision. He had mentioned as early as 1945 how easy it would be to build a house entirely of large sheets of glass. It was not the virtuosity that appealed but the fundamental simplicity. His love of hard, mechanically precise materials was the basis of his particular aesthetic. In the Farnsworth House the maker's name on the steel sections was seen as an affront to purity and had to be laboriously ground smooth. This architecture essentially depended on steel and glass, even if the inner supporting structure was of concrete.

The second aesthetic sprang from forms developed by Le Corbusier which relied on and exploited the plastic nature of concrete. With the consistency of wet mud when first placed, concrete can take on virtually any form, however free. After a wonderfully inventive period which ended in 1933, Le Corbusier surprisingly received no substantial commissions until after the war, but around 1950 he had, among others, three large and important commissions: first, a block of flats (with ancillary functions) the size of a small town at Marseilles; second, a pilgrimage church at Ronchamp; third, the design of a new capital for

■ Right New York's Seagram Building (1956–8), designed by Mies van der Rohe with Philip C Johnson. This architectural prototype was adapted in various ways for office buildings throughout the world.

■ Left The Guggenheim Museum, New York, designed by Frank Lloyd Wright and completed in 1959. The exterior echoes the spiral ramp inside – the framework on which the interior space hangs.

Above right Le Corbusier's Unité d'Habitation (1946–52) in Marseilles, France. The sculptural elements, seen here on the roof of the building, are in marked contrast to the more grid-like structure of the façades.

the Punjab at Chandigarh. The Unité d'Habitation (1946–52) at Marseilles, a great cellular block, carries its sculptural elements like a separate world on the roof, whereas the church is pure sculpture – inside and out – studded with jewel-like elements of enamelled steel and stained glass in strong primary colours. No simple rational structure is evident. The building is an abstract assembly of white sculptural forms, emotional rather than rational. In the same spirit, but on a very large scale, is the main group of buildings at Chandigarh, commissioned in 1950 and completed in 1965. The four main government buildings, each a massive and powerfully moulded concrete sculpture, stand isolated and apart in careful relationship to each other on an empty plain.

The work of Le Corbusier had a wide influence during the 1950s. In London, the Royal Festival Hall (1956) owes him some debt, and in New York the United Nations Building (1949–52) can claim direct descent.

Innovation in Graphics

In the field of graphic design and advertising, the 1950s was a period of considerable innovation and experimentation. This was the decade in which the largely European pre-war revolution in the visual arts finally filtered through to the commercial world. Movements such as Surrealism, Abstractionism and the Bauhaus came to influence the work of art directors and graphic artists around the world, largely as a result of the wartime exodus of talented designers from Germany and Eastern Europe.

If there was one characteristic of graphics in the 1950s to distinguish it from the work produced in the preceding decade it was the use of a single, powerful visual idea that united both image and text. The introduction of photolithography enabled full-colour photographs to be easily reproduced for the first time, while the design of new typefaces, notably Helvetica and Univers, produced a leaner, consistent, less cluttered look.

The desirability of some goods was conveyed by advertisements showing the product seemingly floating in white space. A 1956 advertisement by the US company Knoll Associates showed only an object wrapped in brown paper: on the following page one discovered that the contents of the package were a model seated on a new design of pedestal chair. Advertisements for foodstuffs such as Campbell's soup and Del Monte canned fruits, while less economical in design, made imaginative use of large-scale cut-out pictures and incorporated menu ideas and product information as well as hard-selling slogans in the text. Packaging likewise adopted the more economic visual style, with food cans often featuring colour photographs of the contents, or sometimes elegant lines, such as the 'trellis' design used on packets of Jacob's Cream Crackers.

Britain's first television commercial was screened in 1955. It showed a pack of Gibbs SR toothpaste breaking out of a block of ice. British advertising agencies took some time to come to terms with the new medium, although a notable campaign of the early years was the launch of Babycham, using some remarkable animation by André Sarrut.

As television gradually established itself, magazine publishers responded by placing more emphasis on photography, leading to the success of magazines such as *Look* and *Life* in the United States and *Picture Post* in Britain. In the United States *McCalls* and *Esquire* both went even further, taking on distinguished designers to create covers and picture spreads aiming for dramatic impact: text broke out of its rigid column format to 'sprinkle' from the hands of models or to undu-

■ **Above** Advertisements for packaged foods often presented the housewife with a number of recipe ideas.

■ **Right** This press advertisement for Jayson menswear was one of many that used white space to enhance desirability.

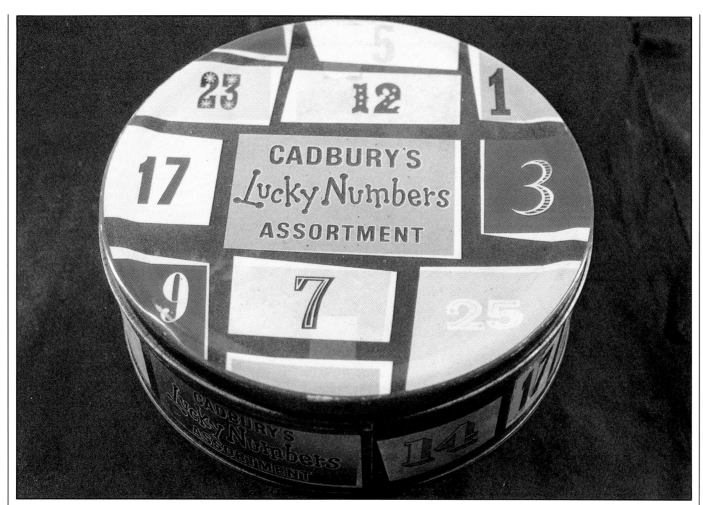

■ **Above** One of the most striking visual styles of the decade was the 'collage' look exemplified by this Cadbury's biscuit tin.

■ **Left** Photography came to dominate the magazine world during the 1950s.

late across the page as it followed the contours of a picture.

Book covers and internal designs were changing more slowly. While Penguin paperbacks in Britain retained their rather plain, generally unillustrated covers throughout the 1950s, in the United States the New York designer Alvin Lustig was commissioned to create a series of striking montage covers for New Directions, a literary publishing company.

In the movies, where publicity material had traditionally been dominated by portrait-style pictures of actors and actresses, director Otto Preminger employed the designer Saul Bass to develop unified posters, advertisements, logos and titles for a series of films. One of the first results was a disturbing angular figure of an outstretched hand for the movie *The Man with the Golden Arm* (1955).

An increasing number of major companies were likewise attracted by the idea of having a unified graphic design. Corporate identity was still a relatively new notion, although the Italian company Olivetti had started to implement a comprehensive design as early as 1947. Outstanding examples in the late 1950s were Paul Rand's design for IBM, in 1956, and his electronic circuitry logo tor Westinghouse four years later.

Shapes and Patterns

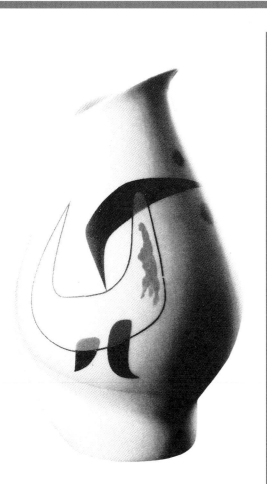

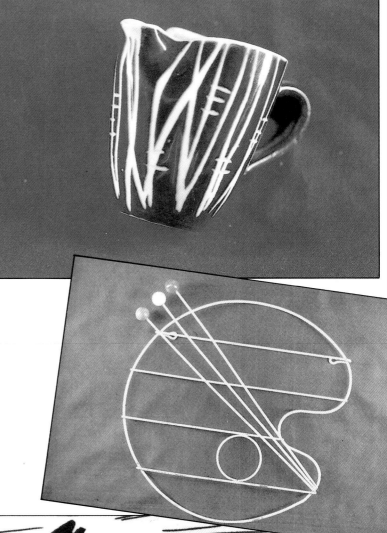

■ The boomerang and kidney shapes appeared in numerous forms throughout the 1950s, ranging from chairs (**far right**) to tables – here printed onto a Ridgway Potteries 'Homemaker' plate (**right**). The strong black and white background of this dish is taken a step further on this jug (**top right**), with its zebra pattern recalling Africa and primitive cultures.

■ **Above right** The palette shape, with its associations with Paris and art, was a popular motif, here shown in the form of a wall ornament.

■ **Above** This Rosenthal vase, featuring a design by Klaus Bendixen, shows the influence of Surrealist art as well as that of primitive cave drawings.

Fashion's New Freedom

The late 1950s saw an end to the era of strict tailoring in fashion and the start of a new freedom and informality. US department stores continued to send buyers to France and Italy, where they would seek out the lesser known – and hence cheaper – couturiers . . . until those couturiers finally realized that there was nothing to prevent them from setting up their own lines to be sold worldwide.

Nevertheless, although their interest in the European fashion scene continued (Britain could not quite yet be described as a leading setter of styles, despite talents such as Hardy Amies and Norman Hartnell), US designers were gaining confidence and, more important, transatlantic recognition. In fact, by the end of the decade clothing had become the third largest industry in the United States, and had sufficient 'pull' to lure designers such as Main R. Bocher back home from Paris; he continued working under his French fashion-house name of Mainbocher.

It was a very active time in Paris. Fashion houses were rising and falling – the notable new arrivals were Hubert de Givenchy, Pierre Cardin and, in 1958, Yves Saint Laurent. The most significant event, however, was the return of Gabrielle 'Coco' Chanel, who opened her new fashion house in 1954 after an absence of 14 years. She had a profound effect on women's fashion: by the end of the 1950s her soft elegant suits were to be seen everywhere. The success of Chanel's clothes lay in their comfort and the ease with which they could be worn – in sharp contrast with the stiffer, more structured garments prevalent at the time. Chanel also led the move towards fashion-house diversification. Besides her famous perfume,

Chanel Number 5, she produced costume jewellery, notably her long gilt chains. Many other houses followed this trend, producing goods such as belts and scarves which satisfied people's desire to own a more affordable designer item.

The move towards looser garments was taken a step further by the Spanish designer Balenciaga, who in 1957 produced a straight tunic-like dress which became known as the chemise or sack dress. Such garments became very popular, and from them was born Yves Saint Laurent's successful 'Trapeze' line in 1958. Many ready-to-wear manufacturers copied this style, but unfortunately did not realize – or care – that it had to be cut very well and from high-quality material if it was to be flattering; their use of cheap material and the basically tubular shape they cut were responsible for the fact that the style did not translate well to the mass-production end of the market.

During the latter half of the 1950s a fashion revolution that would not come to the boil until the following decade was, as it were, bubbling under. The focus of this incipient revolution was Britain, which up until now had not been particularly imaginative. All this was set to change when, in 1955, Mary Quant opened her boutique, Bazaar, in London's King's Road. Quant designed for the young and adventurous. She used strong, unusual colours – such as lime-green and pink – and put them together in strange combinations. Her clothes were uninhibited, contrasting strongly with the rather more restrained designs of the other British fashion setters. But it was this very unconventionality which made them so appealing and which would set the scene for the flamboyance of the 1960s.

■ **Right** In the late 1950s hemlines rose and fashion found a new freedom. Full skirts were still popular although a looser, less structured look was beginning to gain acceptance.

■ **Above** The move towards straighter and looser garments can be seen in this 'Trapeze' line dress designed by Yves Saint Laurent for Christian Dior in 1958.

■ **Above right** Fashion for men still had a long way to go although manufacturers recognized that for leisure men wanted style as well as comfort.

■ **Right** The return of 'Coco' Chanel (pictured here) had a profound effect on fashion and her elegant suits soon became classics, popular throughout the world for their comfort as well as style.

All About Eve

The hourglass shape proved a very popular look for women in the 1950s – particularly US and Italian film stars, helped no doubt by Howard Hughes' cantilevered, pointed brassiere. Marilyn Monroe (**left**) and Sophia Loren (**below**).

■ The similarity is unmistakable: Jayne Mansfield (**below**) and Barbie (**left**), the grown-up doll launched in 1959 with a host of accessories – ranging from a boyfriend to a beauty salon.

CALIFORNIA 56
NBB 851

Italian Cool

The only serious challenge to US cultural supremacy in the late 1950s came from Italy, which surfaced from the destruction of the 1940s with a very strong 'look' encompassing clothes, furniture, interior design and, as we shall see, the cinema.

The Italian fashion market was based in Milan, Rome and Florence. From these cities designers such as Emilio Pucci, Simonetta, Fabiani and Valentino set out to take their designs to the world. Emilio Pucci spearheaded the push into the United States with his bright, almost psychedelic patterns used for casual clothes and sportswear. This was a field in which the Italians excelled, producing chic well cut knitwear, such as off-the-shoulder jumpers, as well as ponchos and tight-fitting ankle-length trousers and ski pants. They experimented with very bright colours, such as lemon-yellow, the vividness of which was made possible by the new synthetic materials.

The 'Italian look' spread swiftly, and was even taken up by the young of the working classes. The style was introduced to Britain by Cecil Gee, who had a chain of stores in which he sold cheap off-the-peg copies of suits by designers such as Brioni. These suits had a rather squat look, with short tight trousers and 'bum-freezer' jackets; to complete the look, long pointed shoes were worn – along with stiletto heels, Italy's main contribution to the international shoe market.

Italian furniture and interior design were also popular all over the world. As early as the late 1940s, Italian designers such as Carlo Mollino and Enrico Rava had been producing very original furniture, and the 1950s saw the continuation and development of their innovation. The Italians aimed for a simple pure 'line', as demonstrated by pieces as diverse as a Visetta or Mirella sewing machine, Artelucce lamp or Olivetti desk. Interior designers such as Gio Ponti had great influence, and their classic designs were shown to the world at exhibitions such as the Milan Triennales in 1951, 1954 and 1957.

There is no doubt that by the end of the 1950s it was cool to be continental – and coolest of all to be Italian. Young people throughout Europe and the United States were riding Vespa or Lambretta motor-scooters, wearing Italian-style slacks and sports shirts, and meeting in coffee bars to sip Italian Espresso or Cappuccino coffee and listen to pop songs such as 'Che Sera, Sera'. In the cinema, Italian stars such as Sophia Loren and Gina Lollobrigida were at the height of their success, making the hourglass shape – already much used by Italian designers for anything from vases to chairs – a model for women worldwide.

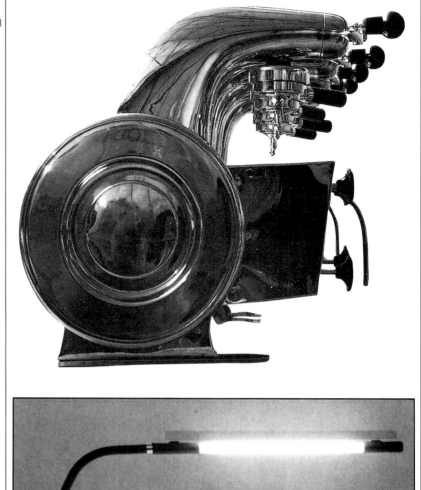

■ **Top** A coffee machine any Espresso bar owner would be proud of: Gio Ponti's sleek chrome creation was manufactured by La Pavoni.

■ Gino Sarfatti's light for Artelucce, 1955 (**left**), and the Giacomo brothers' 1950 'Tubino' light (**above**) show the Italian preoccupation with simplicity and pure lines.

■ **Right (inset)** Gio Ponti was one of the most famous Italian architects/designers. He received worldwide acclaim thanks to the Milan Triennales in 1951, 1954 and 1957.

■ **Right** Vespa Motor Scooters became an international symbol of Italian style that could be afforded by the young.

your

pipe the piping on h..
pockets, not to mention his
India madras shirt,
high-rise socks
and lightweight cap

*Available from Whitehouse & Hardy,
Miami Beach and New York City*

PHOTOGRAPH BY RICHARD LITWIN

Jet-Age Dreams

Nowhere was the brashness of the 1950s more apparent than in US car design: while the Old and New worlds grew closer in many areas, in this field they were poles apart. In the United States cars were more than just a means of getting from A to B: they were an outward sign of the inner self and a useful way of telling the world how successful you were. The bigger the car and the more up-to-date the model, the better its driver was doing – 'conspicuous consumption' was the byword.

Styling was everything: it was the look that sold the car, not the engineering. Buyers had faith in what was under the hood and anyway had no interest in pistons and crank shafts: what they wanted to buy was a dream. In 1948 Harley Earl of General Motors took a design detail from the Lockheed P-38 Lightning aircraft and used it on a range of Cadillacs to give them, in his words, 'graceful bulk'. This design detail was the tail fin, and it was to dominate US automobile styling throughout the 1950s.

By 1953, everyone in the United States who really needed a car had already bought one, so the automobile companies realized that if they were to keep up their sales figures they would have to change their styling more often. The great idea was to use design features so extreme that they would date quickly. This concept – an annual change of model – was so successful that, between 1953 and the end of 1955, US citizens had spent $65 billion on new cars.

1955 marked a watershed in US car design. Out went any vestige of the old rounded look and in came the angular, streamlined shape. Cars were low-slung and bulky, with wrap-around windscreens, wide grilles and a host of chrome features – as well as those all-important tail fins.

Chevrolets, which up until now had been looked upon as rather dull but dependable cars, re-appeared in bright new colours with sharp tail fins and big powerful engines. Chrysler, not to be left behind, unveiled its new 'Forward Look', designed by Virgil Exner, the same year. And while some designers, such as Raymond Loewy, condemned these extravagantly designed cars as 'jukeboxes on wheels', the public loved them.

The contrast with European car design at this time could not have been more startling. While 'the bigger the better' was the cry of US consumers, Europeans looked for economy – in size as well as in price. Germany's Volkswagen Beetle – initially designed by Dr Ferdinand Porsche in 1935 but not really in common use until the 1950s – was a prime example of this. At the same time that US companies were advertising 'More For Your Money' the slogan for the VW Beetle was 'Think Small'. This feeling was taken up in 1957 in Italy with the launch of the Fiat 500 and in Britain with the Austin 850, better known as the Mini-Minor, in 1959.

The Mini was designed by Alec Issigonis. Its focus on economy of running was strongly influenced by the fact that the Suez Crisis of 1956 had caused Britain's oil supplies to be cut by 20 per cent. Its small, neat design ignored all US trends – unlike the Triumph Herald of the same year, which had tail fins, albeit only small ones. Like the Beetle, the Mini sold very badly in the United States but extraordinarily well throughout Europe.

These differences in styling and in economic and comfort requirements had a great deal to do with geography. In 1956 41,000 miles (66,000km) of new roads were built in the United States, and so automobiles were designed to drive long dis-

■ **Below** The Boeing 707 – the first jet to be offered to commercial airlines. It was given its sleek look by Walter Darwin Teague.

■ While Americans believed bigger was better, as this Eldorado Brougham shows (**below right**), Europeans were thinking small, with cars such as the Mini Minor (**right**) proving to be a runaway success.

■ **Inset right** Cadillac introduced aircraft-inspired tail fins to the world in 1948 and set a styling trend that was copied by almost every other US car. The Cadillac fins reached their acme in 1959.

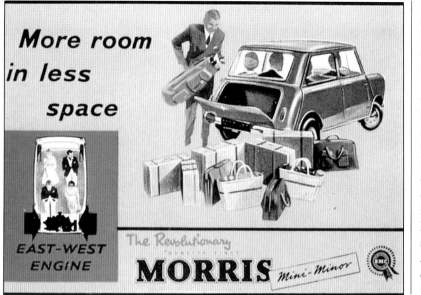

tances on wide straight roads, their occupants enjoying comfort throughout the long journey times involved. By contrast, in Britain, for example, it would not be until 1959 that the first motorway (freeway) was built.

People's ideas about distance in the late 1950s were changed by a far more wide-reaching event than anything surface transport could offer: the arrival of jet passenger aircraft. These made air travel faster, cheaper and much more comfortable. In 1955 the Boeing 707 became the first jet to be offered to commercial airlines, and in 1958 it came into use. To make it conform to popular ideas of how a jet aircraft should look, Boeing hired Walter Darwin Teague, an industrial designer, to give the aircraft a sleeker, faster appearance, while at the same time designing a corporate identity for the airline as a whole. The jet age had arrived.

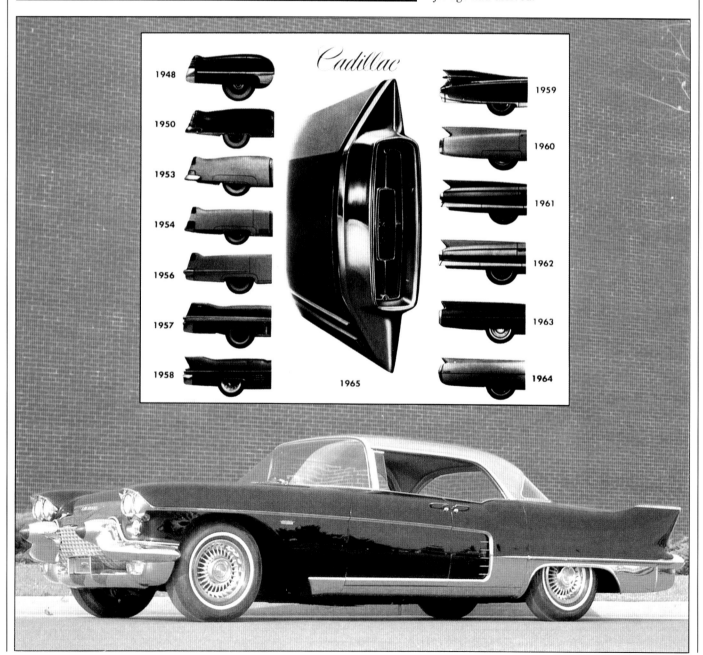

SIGN OF GOOD TASTE...EVERYWHERE

Sketched at famous Varadero Beach ... Coca-Cola adds to the moment of fun

COLORFUL CUBA, TOO, ENJOYS..."THE FAVORITE OF THE WORLD."

Apparently there is something universally right about the special appeal of Coca-Cola to human tastes and thirsts. ● In more than 100 countries today, the taste of Coke is so well liked, the good taste of Coke so well recognized, that over 58 million times each day someone, somewhere, enjoys Coca-Cola. ● *Have a Coke* ... so good in taste, in such good taste.

■ Even Coca-Cola worked hard to identify their products with leisure-time pursuits (**above**).

Shorter working hours and more money in people's pockets, coupled with cheaper and better systems of transportation, ensured that more people than ever before could afford to go on holiday. In some areas, such as the Mediterranean coastline of France and Spain, a booming tourist industry began to alter the character of seaside resorts as they strove to cater for the growth of package holidays – a trend that was to accelerate out of control in the 1970s and 1980s.

The World's Most Modern Air Fleet

AIR FRANCE
The Luxury World wide Airline

skin needs NIVEA

smoothness

■ Cosmetics manufacturers encouraged the sales of sun-related beauty products with images of health and fresh air (**above** and **left**).

■ Europe – in particular Paris, Rome and London – was heavily promoted in glossy US magazines **Top left**.

A mass-produced Beatles tray, c. 1964.

1960-1965

Spend, Spend, Spend

If the 1940s had been a period of tightening belts and the 1950s a time of letting them out, then the 1960s can be credited with having invented the elasticated waistband. 'Consume!' was the message, and it was delivered and received loud and clear. Money spoke. Built-in obsolescence was no longer a rumour: here in the shop windows were paper dresses and cardboard chairs designed to last as long as the consumer's interest. 'Throw-away aesthetics' is what P. Reyner Banham, the writer and critic, dubbed the phenomenon, but nonetheless these aesthetics have lasted.

Much of the change in attitudes and values between the 1950s and the 1960s can be credited to the increasing influence of the 'younger generation'. By the late 1950s youth had become acceptable; not only did young people account for a larger proportion of the population than ever before, they also had more leisure time and – importantly – more money. To enlightened youth, rules, regulations, traditions, authorities – even laws – were no longer to be adhered to with blind reverence. In the place of obedience came questions and the notion of the right to choose. Those choices inevitably concerned fashion and music, the two areas that blossomed under youth patronage: the sound of the Beatles could be heard down every corridor and the miniskirt shocked parents the world over.

A profusion of channels of communication – in the form of magazines, newspapers, films and television – served the dual purpose of feeding off and feeding out new ideas around the world. In 1962 the first communications satellite, Telstar, was launched; and by the end of the 1960s most industrialized nations broadcast colour television. The first half of the 1960s saw the establishment of many new glossy magazines including *The Sunday Times Colour Supplement* (Britain), *Lui* (France), *Twen* (Germany) and *Nova* (Britain). It also saw the demise of some old favourites, such as the *Saturday Evening Post* (US). In the new magazines the reader was presented with a vast array of brightly coloured images of the very latest fashions and designs.

Mobility, both geographical and social, became a real possibility. A network of internal airplane flights across the United States and international flights throughout Europe and around the world gave many more people the opportunity to travel to faraway places. In Britain and other European countries where relatively rigid social structures had existed, less importance was placed on social class; the heroes and heroines of the 1960s – as chronicled in David Bailey's book *New Box of Pin-Ups* (1965) – were the likes of

Michael Caine and Twiggy, who did nothing to hide their working-class origins. It was not where you came from that was important; it was who you were. 'Personality' was all-important. The United States idolized their youngest-ever president, John F. Kennedy; when he was assassinated on 22 November 1963 everyone in the Western world felt it. Andy Warhol stunned the world with his iconic treatment of the humble soup tin, and as a result rarely had his face out of the newspapers.

Above all, the 1960s was characterized by the feeling that an immense break with the past had been achieved. Clothes, furniture and products all looked newer, brighter and more 'fun'. A need to use and consume pervaded all areas of life. Clearly this could not last. By the middle of the decade consumerism's many faults would be recognized, and issues of more meaningful and lasting values would force themselves onto the agenda – where they would stay until the 1980s.

■ **Top** In 1965 Edward H White II became the first US astronaut to walk in space. White floated in space for 21 minutes on the end of a 7.5m (25ft) tether line before returning safely to his spacecraft, *Gemini IV*.

■ **Above** A Sainsbury's supermarket in the 1960s. The general acceptance of self-service shopping meant that brands increasingly had to fight for attention on the shelf.

■ **Above right** Women's liberation was a burning issue of the early 1960s, under the leadership of dedicated campaigners such as Betty Friedan. It was also the inspiration behind more frivolous images, such as this advertisement for Elliott's boots.

■ **Right** The signing of the Civil Rights Act by L B Johnson and Martin Luther King in 1960. Such an event could not have been foreseen 20 years earlier.

The Young Generation

The 1960s saw the recognition and establishment of a distinct youth culture. The questioning, and subsequent challenging, of generally accepted views on sex, religion and politics began to take concrete form as the decade progressed. The frustrations and partially unresolved needs of the teenagers and rebels of the 1950s found outlets which were most evident in the music and fashion of the time. Young people could no longer be classed as either children or immature adults; they had a completely different set of values and requirements and, furthermore, they had their own 'gods' to prove it.

The heroes and heroines of young people changed gradually between the 1950s and 1960s. The heroes of the 1950s had been rebellious characters, such as Elvis Presley, Chuck Berry and Little Richard. However, in their wake came gentler, more acceptable pop stars in the form of the Temptations, the Supremes, Tommy Steele and Cliff Richard. Even the Beatles were hardly revolutionary: how much more innocent could you be than wanting to hold someone's hand? The Beatles managed successfully to appeal not only to young people but also to adults, and Beatlemania took off. In Britain their album, 'Please Please Me' was Number 1 for six months during 1963, and at one time in the following year they held all top five places in the US charts. It was in 1964 that the heroes became more like rebels, in the form of the Rolling Stones and other similar bands. Even the Beatles adapted, adopting a sort of 'semi-rebellious' style.

The spending power of young people was undoubtedly crucial in the general acceptance of their values. Young people had more money in their pockets than ever before to spend on the things they wanted, such as records, transistor radios, clothes and posters of their idols. Most young people still lived with their parents yet were earning acceptable wages. Without the overheads and commitments of running a home and family, they had more money to spend on inessential or 'luxury' goods. Manufacturers in the United States were the first to recognize the commercial implications of this new market, in the 1950s; in the succeeding decade those of Europe and the industrialized countries elsewhere followed suit.

Another factor in the greater freedom afforded to most people – particularly the young – was the increase in leisure time. In Britain, the average working week for a manual-labour job before World War II was 48 hours long, but after the war this figure had dropped to 40 hours. One form of entertainment that arrived to fill this new leisure time and appealed particularly to young people was the discotheque. These jazzed-up dance halls provided not only the opportunity to hear the records of the latest pop stars and let out 'generation-gap' frustrations on the dance floor but also the chance to show off the latest fashions.

Perhaps the single most important development to affect the lifestyle of young people was the arrival of oral contraception. The Pill, as it became known, was approved by the United States Food and Drug Administration in 1960 and became available in most other countries soon afterwards. The implications of virtually guaranteed child-free sex meant that nobody had to be forced into marriage and adulthood by unscheduled pregnancies.

■ **Right** The Mods were originally an exclusive group of fashion-conscious men, but by 1963 the term 'Mod' had taken on a much looser meaning and could be applied to most 'tailored' youth fashions of the period. Part of the Mod ritual was the bank holiday motorbike ride down to the south coast of England, seen here in 1964. The obligatory accessories included a Vespa motorbike and a parka jacket.

READY, STEADY, GO!

ASSOCIATED·REDIFFUSION'S TOP **TV** POP SHOW

■ **Left** and **Below** *Ready, Steady, Go!* first shown in 1963, was a television programme for young people. It presented strong pop graphics as well as the very latest in fashion and music. Its compère, Cathy McGowan (**below right**), quickly became a cult heroine.

■ **Right** Rivals of the Mods were the Rockers, a cult group that had a greater affinity with motorbike grease than a tailor's measuring tape. Leather clothes and crash helmets were the trademarks, seen here on a gang of ton-up boys and girls outside London's Dorchester Hotel in 1963.

Pop Stars

■ The pop-music industry – under the patronage of a young generation with pocket money and wages to spend – elevated its moneymakers to the status of movie stars with similar-style press-release photographs. Here, The Supremes (**below**) and The Temptations (**left**) are given the star treatment. The various record companies, such as Columbia and EMI, quickly turned into multi-million dollar concerns.

■ No other group during the 1960s could match The Beatles when it came to catching the hearts and imaginations of all generations (**right**). After their successful conquest of the British market, their sell-out tour of the United States (1964) ensured a far wider audience.

■ In marked contrast to the milder-mannered Beatles, The Rolling Stones adopted a more rebellious image epitomized by their scruffier clothing (**right**). The pop industry and its stars fed other businesses, not least the magazine industry (**above**).

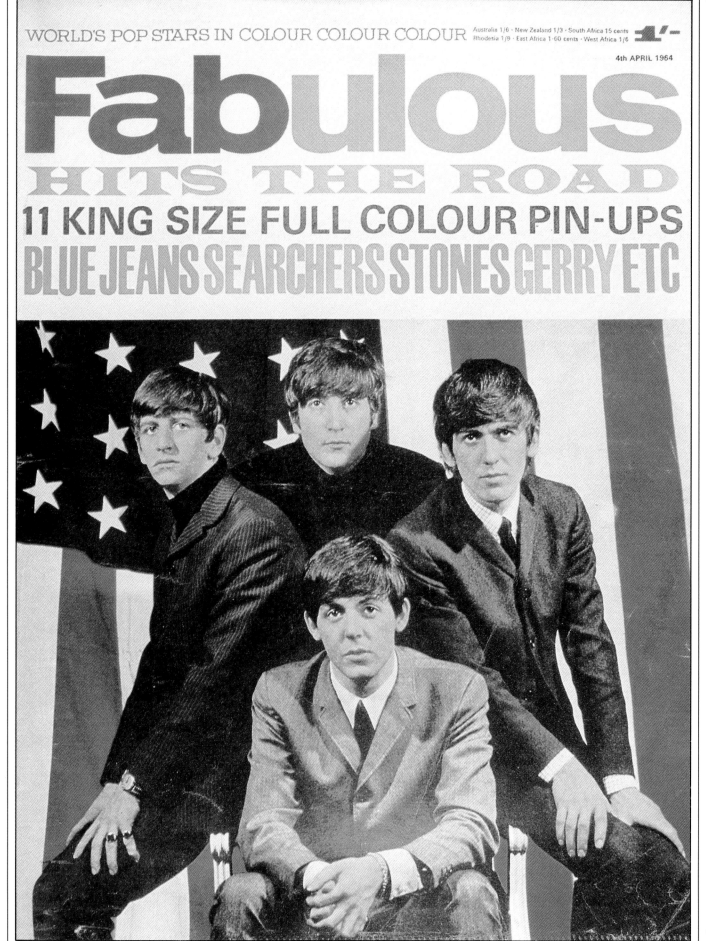

WORLD'S POP STARS IN COLOUR COLOUR COLOUR Australia 1/6 · New Zealand 1/3 · South Africa 15 cents
Rhodesia 1/9 · East Africa 1·60 cents · West Africa 1/6 1'-

4th APRIL 1964

Fabulous
HITS THE ROAD
11 KING SIZE FULL COLOUR PIN-UPS
BLUE JEANS SEARCHERS STONES GERRY ETC

Dressing Up

Fashion was affected as much as any other area of design by the changing attitudes and values of the 1950s and 1960s. It has been said that women's hemlines during the 1960s served as a barometer of contemporary attitudes: when the consumeristic 'Swinging Sixties' were at their height, women's hemlines were likewise; when people began to develop some conscience about their lifestyles, the midi- and maxiskirts made their appearance. Above all, fashion in the 1960s tended to encourage exhibitionism. Miniskirts, lurid colours and see-through dresses were all geared to showing off women's – on rare occasion men's – bodies. Gaudy accessories, such as perspex rings and earrings and gold chain-belts, helped to get the message across.

Traditionally, strict rules had dictated what was worn and when. 'Casuals', for wearing during the daytime, were very distinct from formal evening wear. Similarly, the types of fabrics used were often applied only to specific types of clothing. The 1960s saw the abandonment of these traditional rules, and it became perfectly reasonable to wear the same outfit to work as for an evening out. Many of the fabrics previously restricted to evening wear, such as velvets and satins, were used extensively for all types of clothing. In addition to existing fabrics, many unusual materials entered the clothes designer's vocabulary, including PVC and, on a limited scale, metal.

Whereas it had been Paris and the large couturiers who in the 1950s had dictated clothes fashion, in the early 1960s London sprang to prominence with the emergence of a small group of designers and their boutiques. Most notable of these was Mary Quant, who had opened her boutique, Bazaar, in 1955. However, it was not until the early 1960s that her influence was widely felt. She is credited with having introduced the mini skirt, and 1965 was the unofficial year of its glory. Other designers who established their careers at this time were John Bates (the designer of Diana Rigg's wardrobe in *The Avengers*), Ossie Clark (Quorum), Barbara Hulanicki (Biba) and Betsey Johnson. The key to the success of many of these designers was that they first discovered the youth market and then, second, catered for it. Many of them, notably Barbara Hulanicki, produced exciting clothes at a price that most people could afford.

Paris attempted to fight back by concentrating on ready-to-wear clothes. Designers such as Pierre Cardin and Andrés Courrèges produced media-grabbing collections that took 1960s themes to extremes. In 1964 Courrèges presented a space-age series of clothes that proved influential in establishing white and silver as *the* colours of the season. In the same year he introduced trouser-suits into his collection, and these subsequently entered mainstream fashion on a large scale.

For men there was refinement rather than any real innovation in fashion during the early 1960s. Suits became more tightly fitting, and Chelsea boots became fashionable. In Britain the Mods began as a minority group deeply concerned with their immaculate appearance, but from 1963 onwards they received national coverage and showed that men could care about the clothes they wore, an attitude that was to allow real changes as the decade progressed. Conversely, some pop groups, in particular the Rolling Stones, cultivated a rebellious attitude that was reflected in their unconventional, scruffy clothing.

■ **Below** Joe Loss demonstrating the 'March of the Mods' dance in 1964.

■ **Right (main picture)** Audrey Hepburn in *Breakfast at Tiffany's* (1961). Long black gloves and heavy black eyeliner were essential for evening wear.

■ **Right (inset)** The development of new manmade fabrics affected men's clothing as much as women's wear. This tight-fitting 'Italian' suit was made from 100 per cent terylene.

■ **Far right (inset)** A page from the 1965 Sears catalogue. The design of these clothes and the white boots owes much to Courrèges' collection of 1964.

'TERYLENE': HIGH STYLE, SNUG FIT

Didn't want Janet to see me, sure to return ring if found out accidentally engaged to Diana night before. Bound to be scene. Thought cornered, as narrow alley, no way out. Stroke of luck, wearing suit in 'Terylene'. Wouldn't get torn, frayed, generally creased if squeezed self into narrow opening high up wall. So did so. Could sponge down after.

Shops and Shopping

With the arrival of more money in people's pockets to spend on both essentials and inessentials – first in the United States from the late 1940s and then in other industrialized countries from the early 1950s – shops and shopping were transformed. Not only did the goods on offer represent a display of new technological achievement, the very shops themselves were transformed. 'Retail productivity' was the buzz phrase of the period, and retailers devised many schemes to cut running costs while still keeping the customers buying. Gordon Selfridge had realized early the importance of making shopping a pleasurable experience when he said of his department store: 'This is not a shop – it's a community centre.' Now other retailers began increasingly to agree.

The affluence and spending power of the 1950s ensured that the retailing industry was transformed so as to entertain the 'extra' money that was around. It was during the 1960s and early 1970s that the shopping mall took off as a retailing phenomenon, particularly in the United States. In 1960 there were 4,500 malls in the United States, and they accounted for approximately 14 per cent of the country's retail sales; 15 years later the relevant figures had leapt to 16,400 malls and 33 per cent.

Unlike the case in most European countries, not only did the United States have the space to build such vast complexes but also people had the cars to get to them. Following in the tradition of the general trading store, the mainstay of the mall was the general food store, of both chain and individual units: by 1966, 95 per cent of food was sold through such stores. In the United States and other countries, self-service became an increasingly popular and cost-efficient means of retailing, helped not only by improved refrigeration and dehydration but also by improved packaging materials, such as cheap polythene.

In Europe, the possibility of building vast shopping malls was a less serious proposition in the 1960s, some countries, especially France, preferring hypermarkets instead. These were self-service supermarkets which, like the malls, were usually positioned on the outskirts of town. Small-scale versions of the US mall did materialize in the form of shopping precincts, particularly in the new towns which were springing up around the major cities, but these were designed for the pedestrian rather than for the motorist. In Britain, in particular, the chain or 'multiple' stores, with their strong individual identities dreamed up in design departments, dominated all areas of retailing during the 1960s. Most notable of these was Sainsbury's, who ensured quality throughout the selling process, a belief that was applied as much to interiors, layouts and packaging as to the quality of the food.

The 1960s witnessed too the establishment of 'bargain stores', which provided an outlet for manufacturers' obsolescent overstocks. These stores sold anything from razors to washing machines, and were laid out as warehouse-like interiors with checkouts. In Europe, the rise in the number of boutiques and chain clothing stores opened up a market that had hitherto been dominated by department stores.

▌Right and far right Self-service supermarkets meant that packs had to appeal to the shopper rather than to the grocer. The OMO pack is a particularly blatant example of attention-grabbing design.

▌Below right As well as shopping through the growing number of mail-order companies, housewives could buy products in the comfort of their own homes at shopping 'parties'. Tuppaware is a company making plastic kitchen containers and other domestic items. It has always concentrated on this technique of retailing.

▌Below A pedestrian shopping precinct in Stockholm, built in the 1960s. Similar shopping precincts were being created throughout Europe during this period – particularly in Britain, where they constituted the core of many of the new towns.

Pop Culture

The affluence that swept the United States from the early 1950s onwards – with Europe not far behind – meant the mass-manufacture not only of cheap 'popular' products but also of anything from television programmes and advertisements to comics and throw-away canned drinks. Such items depended on instant appeal – usually to encourage their purchase – and so often used bright colours and gimmicks for effect. Such commercial impact, which during the 1960s became increasingly influenced by market research techniques, was designed to be consumed immediately and forgotten after use.

While Pop undoubtedly aimed at unthinking gut reactions, it was not long before it found willing devotees in more intellectual circles. An appreciation of Pop objects and imagery was first voiced by the Independent Group at the Institute of Contemporary Arts (ICA) in London in the middle 1950s. This group of respected writers, artists and architects included P. Reyner Banham, Eduardo Paolozzi, Richard Hamilton and Alison and Peter Smithson. Influenced by US as well as British Pop, artists such as Paolozzi made collages out of commercial images, the most reproduced example of which was Hamilton's *Just What is it That Makes Today's Home So Different, So Appealing?* (1956). Advertisements for vacuum cleaners and radios were being used to create images worthy of gallery space.

In the United States, Robert Rauschenberg and Jasper Johns (with their interest in the work of Marcel Duchamp) were early to appreciate throw-away three-dimensional objects such as coke bottles. More committed exponents of Pop Art were Andy Warhol and Roy Lichtenstein. Warhol worked originally as a commercial artist, thereby bridging the gap between popular and fine art. Both artists drew on comics for inspiration, but it was Warhol's ironic treatment of supermarket goods that underlined the potency of Pop culture during this period. It is interesting to note that such democratic subject matter was popular for posters at this time.

The cross-fertilization of ideas between popular culture and fine art was completed when the latter began to affect the former. Yves Saint Laurent had fashionable society wearing Mondrian dresses in 1965 and Pop Art dresses decorated with comic strips a year later. However, it was Op Art – the use of patterns to create an optical illusion – that was widely used on popular products. The patterns first seen in the paintings of Victor Vasarely and Bridget Riley found their way onto many graphic and fabric designs.

The term 'pop' was applied in other areas, particularly those of youth interest such as music and clothes: pop music, pop groups and pop clothes all implied youthful, easily digestible fun. By the middle of the 1960s the term had shifted in meaning from 'popular' to 'fashionable' and could be applied to any object, person or event whose appeal was based on instant impact.

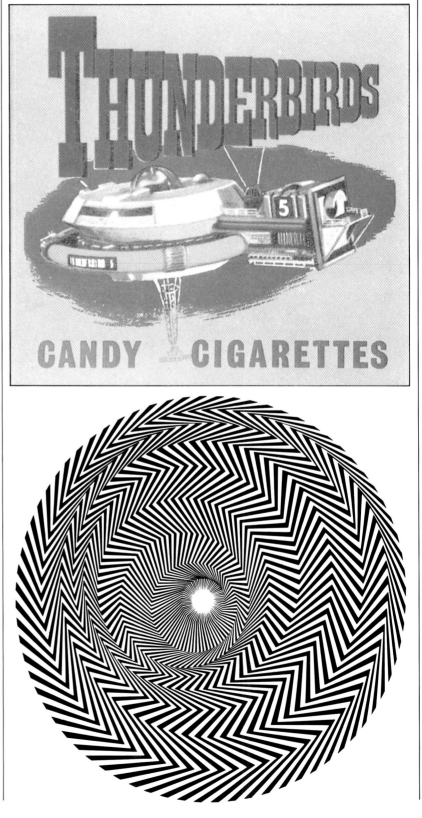

■ **Below** Television was an important contributor to Pop culture.

■ **Bottom** *Blaze 1* (c. 1963), by Bridget Riley. Together with Victor Vasarely, Riley pioneered the use of optical illusion for visual effect (Op Art).

■ **Below and right** The products on offer to the consumer had never been so varied or so bountiful. It took Andy Warhol to give the humble soup can the status of an icon. This is one of several depictions of Campbell's soup can which Warhol did in 1962.

Pictorial Explosion

If the 1950s was a period of experimentation in graphic design, the 1960s witnessed a veritable explosion, as the age of mass communication became a reality and Pop culture propagated a million copies of every image or slogan. Pop influence in graphic design was largely derived from Pop Art, which had had its roots in the mid-1950s in Britain and soon had achieved popularity on the other side of the Atlantic, feeding on images of US commerce and entertainment such as comic strips, packaging and the images of star entertainers. By the mid-1960s, the mesmerising line patterns of Op Art would be making their impact on graphic design, as well as in fashion.

During the early 1960s the most prevalent image in London was of the Union Jack, which found its way onto every kind of accessory, from mugs to badges to shopping bags. It was soon joined as a popular symbol by group portraits of the Beatles, as the Fab Four swiftly rose to megastar status. Their second album, *With the Beatles*, released in 1963 (released in 1964 in the United States as *The Beatles' Second Album*), represented the introduction of what was to become one of the most important media for graphic art in the 1960s: the record sleeve. Photographed by Robert Freeman, it showed the disembodied heads of the Fab Four floating on a dark background.

Another new medium for the graphic artist was the T-shirt, which was soon sporting pictures of Che Guevara and Uncle Sam, among other popular heroes or villains.

In the early 1960s, magazines in Britain took on a new striking visual 'black and white' style, with magazines like *Queen*, *Vogue* and *Nova* making use of the new techniques of photo-lithography to bend, twist and stretch type around the pictures on the page. It was also the era of a new style of fashion photography in which photographers like David Bailey and Brian Duffy for the first time captured models in seemingly unposed 'action' pictures. With the new style came to Britain a new species of magazine – the Sunday colour supplement. *The Sunday Times* launched its magazine in 1962, followed within three years by the *Sunday Telegraph* and the *Observer*. These supplements were devoted almost entirely to the purveying of consumer goods, whether through glossy advertisements or editorial features that nurtured a new interest in design.

Advertising had entered a new, more thoughtful phase by the 1960s. The US agency Doyle Dane Bernach's famous 'Think Small' ad for the Volkswagen Beetle in 1960 typified a style of advertising that replaced the hard-sell with stimulating use of images and thoughtful copy. Major changes in packaging came about with the growing predominance of supermarkets. While manufacturers' products had to assume strong, colourful visuals in order to generate brand identity and so attract the attention of the housewife, supermarket chains like Sainsbury's and International Stores began to produce 'own-label' goods, often in very simple, unadorned packaging.

One other area that saw significant changes in graphic design was that of the book cover. In the United States designer Rudolph de Harak produced more than 300 book covers for McGraw-Hill based on a common typography and grid. Penguin soon followed suit, under the guidance of Germano Facetti, and began also to feature sketches, drawings and photomontage on its front covers.

■ **Below** By the early 1960s, a new style of photography captured models in poses that were sometimes animated, and frequently unorthodox.

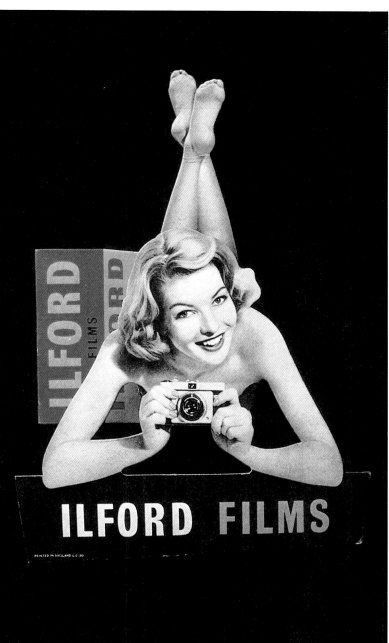

■ **Below** Sunday colour supplements introduced a new medium for advertisements, which were often juxtaposed with articles that confronted urgent social issues.

SAINSBURY'S CORN FLAKES

■ **Above** Supermarkets introduced own-label goods in simple, consistent packaging.

THE SUNDAY TIMES *magazine*

FEBRUARY 21, 1965

The Multiplyin Bunnies

PETER STUYVESANT

Peter Stuyvesant FILTER 20

the international passport to smoking pleasure

so much more to enjoy

■ **Above** The imagery employed in cigarette advertising often exploited the allure of jet-set lifestyles.

International Interiors

The influence of Italian and Scandinavian styling on European and US furniture and interior design during the 1950s continued into the early 1960s. The growth in the number of colour magazines ensured that more people than ever before were exposed to 'designed' goods. Any home that had pretentions to being 'design conscious' contained, for example, ergonomically sound Scandinavian chairs and stainless-steel cutlery, and Italian lighting and glass. The open-plan type of interior arrangement was widely accepted, and many property developers used it for their new homes, particularly for combining living rooms and dining rooms.

In the United States, Scandinavian Modern had had an enormous impact during the 1950s but, from the early 1960s onward, furniture and other items of interior design began to take on a more subdued, international flavour. This style could combine not only Italian, Scandinavian and US contemporary pieces of furniture but also pre-war designs of the Bauhaus period, now back in production thanks to some enlightened companies, such as Knoll International. As far as home-grown US design was concerned, both Knoll (under the direction of Florence Knoll) and Charles Eames, working for the company Herman Miller, continued to produce furniture of 'good taste' rather than of innovatory design.

In Europe, Italian companies such as Cassina, Tecno and Kartell dominated furniture design, and Flos and Artemide reigned supreme in the field of lighting. Vico Magistretti's '892' chair, put into production by Cassina in 1963, was typical of the Italian flair for combining elegant shapes with practicability. In the area of plastics design, too, Italy led the field throughout the decade, although the British designer Robin Day's polypropylene chair of 1963, with its injection-moulded seat, dominated the British commercial furniture market.

The wholesale acceptance of so-called 'good design' – deeply influenced by Bauhaus and Corbusier principles – began to be challenged in Europe in the early 1960s. Established showcases of the design industry, such as the Milan Trienniales and the Council of Industrial Design (CoID) in Britain, were criticized for presenting only one view of 'good design' and not taking into consideration also the effects of popular culture.

Furniture outlets remained geared toward marketing traditional designs until the 1960s. The opening of Terence Conran's Habitat shop on the Fulham Road, London, in 1964 was seen as a complete departure in furniture retailing. It stocked not only contemporary designs from home and abroad but also traditional furniture and items of kitchen equipment from countries all over the world. Many of the products on sale were bright and cheerful, and were presented in an informal environment designed to appeal to a younger market.

■ **Right** Chair designed by Olivier Mourgue in 1963. The 1960s saw many adventurous furniture designs, some of which were unlikely ever to appeal to the mass market.

■ **Below right** The 'Arco' light (1962), designed by the Castiglioni brothers and manufactured by Flos. The lamp is made of stainless steel and aluminium, and has a marble base.

■ **Below far right** Bedroom furniture of the early 1960s. Posters were a cheap new way to decorate plain walls.

■ **Left** A formica fitted kitchen on show at Heals in 1965. Bold colours were designed to appeal to younger customers.

Product Design

The mass production of consumer goods accelerated throughout the 1960s: growing demand coupled with improved technology and more cost-efficient means of production meant that the retailing trade had never had it so good. As a result, a wider range of products was available to more people than ever before. For example, by 1967 there were 391 televisions for every 1,000 people in the United States, and 262 televisions for every 1,000 people in Britain.

Such developments, however, brought with them changing attitudes and values. The purchase of a particular brand reflected directly on the consumer how much they were prepared to pay or how much they could afford. Paul Reilly, Director of the Council of Industrial Design (CoID), noted this development in an editorial in May 1960 in *Design* magazine when he wrote: 'Status symbolism and social aspiration have become major factors in design policy . . . Must the consumer now be tailored to suit the product as well as vice versa?'

The 1960s certainly saw the manufacture of many more products that had been designed with the user in mind. The extensive research into ergonomics of the previous decades found many more outlets, from power tools to motorbikes. The drivers' cabs of both the Tokkaido line high-speed

train (put into service by the Japanese National Railways in 1963) and the DAF F2600 truck (built in Holland and put into production in 1964), for example, were designed with comfort and function as their main criteria.

Many of the large international product companies consolidated their design programmes during this time, using either in-house design teams or employing design-consultancy firms to create a corporate image. International Business Machines (IBM) was a major company to institute an integrated design programme which, in the words of its Consultant Director of Design, Eliot Noyes, meant 'consistent use of colour, detail and form'. It applied its rules of design to all its products, including the Selectric typewriter, introduced in 1961 (the first typewriter to use a golf-ball mechanism), and the compact System 360 computer of 1964. P. Reyner Banham, writing in 1963 on the influence of IBM design, said 'the machine that replaces your secretary and sets her free for full-time pre-marital sex, will probably look less like a battery hen-house full of war-surplus W/T equipment than a tastefully two-toned filing cabinet with cooling louvres, discreetly wired to what appears to be a typewriter with ideas above its station'.

Other companies that manufactured 'styled' products included Eastman Kodak and Braun. The Carousel slide projector, designed by Hans Gugelot and put into production in 1961, and the Brownie Vecta, designed by Kenneth Grange three years later, were both innovative Kodak productions not only in terms of their visual design but also in their new approaches to old problems. Braun concentrated on clean, pure outlines for its products, a principle applied to the stereo radiogram and radio designed for the company by Dieter Rams in 1965. Olivetti continued to produce stylish goods, but it was not until the late 1960s, particularly with the work of Ettore Sottsass, that the company produced more striking designs.

■ **Above left** An electric kettle produced by Braun in 1961 under the design direction of Dieter Rams. Together with Hans Gugelot, Rams was responsible for creating the sophisticated styling of Braun products.

■ **Left** The IBM 'System 360' computer, designed by an in-house team under the direction of Eliot Noyes, was released in 1964.

■ **Above right** The 'Courier' shaver designed by Kenneth Grange and manufactured by Henry Milward in 1963. Despite winning various awards, this somewhat phallic product did not sell well.

■ **Right** Stainless steel cutlery designed by David Mellor in 1965.

Plastics Versus Craft

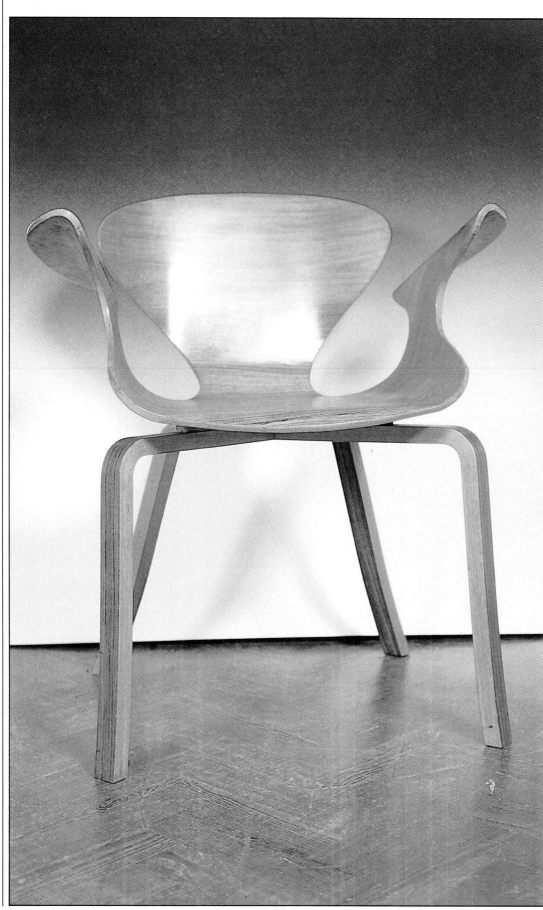

■ New manmade materials inevitably had both supporters and opponents. Blatant exploitation of the properties of plastic in particular, seen here in this inflatable chair (**far right**), went to one extreme. Retaliation came in the form of a craft revival focusing on traditional materials. The moulded plywood chair (**left**), designed by Bernard Lamb in 1966, looked as if it had been crafted in a workshop rather than assembled in a factory.

In some instances, attempts were made to simulate nature using synthetics. 'Nubian' laminated plastic sheet (**below right**), produced by Formica in 1963, tried hard. Glass remained the prerogative of the craft tradition, these goblets (**above right**) being designed by Robert Welch in 1968.

ZETA

The all-colour photo fantasy

Volume 1 No 5 Price 5

Island of the Planet   An exciting new 2 part story   Episode 1– Take me to your leader

Cinema's New Wave

The 1960s was a decade of transition as well as renaissance for the cinema. At the beginning of the decade Hollywood was still caught in the artistic no-man's-land of the 1950s, yet by its end the cinema had become more radical and, instead of concentrating on creating an ideal or fantasy world, was tackling contemporary issues such as war, class barriers, poverty and exploitation. The new topics, hitherto considered too 'dangerous' for the movies, made a strong appeal to an increasingly disaffected youth.

The decade saw massive change in society's values and morals and a swing away from traditional to alternative thinking and lifestyles. All this was echoed in the cinema. Screen violence and sex became accepted so, while Fellini's *La Dolce Vita* (made in the late 1950s but not seen widely until 1960) caused a storm when it first appeared because of its focus on hedonistic Romans living purely for the moment, by the end of the decade their orgies came to be seen as relatively tame.

The depiction of violence likewise changed radically: compare the minute or so of frenzied carnage in Hitchcock's *Psycho* (1960) with the almost ritual violence (shown in slow motion to heighten its effect) of Peckinpah's *The Wild Bunch* (1969) or Hopper's *Easy Rider* (1969). Similarly, the popularity of James Bond, with his penchant for making love to women then casually killing them – all in a very cool, stylized fashion – was a reflection of society.

In the early 1960s the movie industries in Britain and France were in the middle of massive creative upheavals, with the 'Nouvelle Vague' movement in France and the 'New Wave' in Britain. These had started in the late 1950s with films such as *Les Quatres Cents Coups* (France) and *Room at the Top* (Britain), both from 1959. The film makers showed social awareness, and they rejected the studio system in favour of low-budget movies shot on location with natural lighting – hence their rougher finish and 'grainy realism'. They often picked quite controversial subjects – for example, the highly successful British film *A Taste of Honey* (1961), directed by Tony Richardson, dealt with a pregnant schoolgirl and a homosexual. Also, the new film makers rejected the 'star system', instead picking young unknowns (such as Albert Finney) for leading roles.

The success and influence of these films, and of the New Wave and Nouvelle Vague movements, were enormous for, although the movements died out in both Britain and France by 1964, many of the techniques were taken up by the mainstream cinema. They were responsible for making British and French films popular worldwide and for

■ **Below** From comic strip to the big screen: Jane Fonda camps it up as Barbarella in Roger Vadim's 1967 movie based on Jean-Claude Forest's original.

■ **Opposite below** *Easy Rider* (1969) showed what it was like to be a young drop-out in the late-1960s United States. According to one of its stars, Peter Fonda, it was: 'cinéma-vérité in allegory terms'.

■ The decade started with British film-makers showing social awareness with films such as 1962's *A Taste of Honey* (**far right**). Many US studios were still caught up in a sentimental fantasy world, as shown in 1961's *Breakfast at Tiffany's* (**below**).

launching directors such as François Truffaut, Jean-Luc Godard, Karel Reisz and Lindsay Anderson into international celebrity. The British New Wave films also introduced a series of unknown actresses who quickly became very popular in the United States as the vogue for Britishness developed. By 1965 there had been a shift from New Wave to 'Swinging Sixties' movies, and actresses such as Julie Christie and Vanessa Redgrave began to symbolize groovy London to the world.

The large US studios were anxious to cash in on the international taste for Britain, and so poured money into the country – in fact, by 1967–8 they were financing 90 per cent of all British first features. Film makers from all over the world flocked to Britain, with directors such as Michelangelo Antonioni making *Blow-Up* and Truffaut *Fahrenheit 451*, both in 1966. London was where it was at, and movies such as *The Knack* (1965) and *Alfie* (1966) reflect the spirit of freedom everyone aspired to in the 1960s.

Faces of the Decade

tomorrow
angel face dare you
to be seen with
Nothing On

Angel Face's most shameless stroke of genius. A completely new all-in-one make-up so subtly blended that the barest whisper covers and conceals ... so innocently underdressed that only you know it's there. Tomorrow, dare to be seen with Nothing On —you'll get away with it, beautifully.

angel face
NOTHING ON
gives you the wickedest
no-make-up look you've ever worn

a Chesebrough-Pond's beauty product

Trade Mark

the face makers

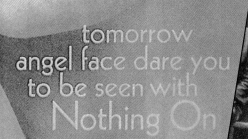

■ The ever-increasing number of channels of communications in the 1960s – from television, films and radios to magazines and newspapers – gave constant exposure to famous people and created new 'celebrities'. Coverage concentrated on personal details, so that the viewer or reader came to feel almost personally acquainted with the stars.

■ To many, Twiggy (**left**) represented the 'poor girl makes good' cliché while nevertheless retaining a certain innocence. Brigitte Bardot (**inset below**), by contrast, was the archetypal 1960s sex kitten.

■ The Beatles rise to fame as depicted in the media (**inset right**) was every teenager's dream. In reality the group's life was one of hard work and constant harassment by devoted fans.

■ John F. Kennedy, seen here on the morning of his inauguration in January, 1961 (**right**), suffered more than most from excessive press coverage. His wife Jackie, later Jackie Onassis, received no mercy after his assassination in 1963.

A 1968 advertisement for cosmetics.

1966-1969

Conscious and Conscience

The enthusiasm that had embraced the mass consumption of goods in the 1950s and the first half of the 1960s was gradually diluted by a spirit of inquiry and soul-searching. Colour television brought into many people's homes vivid pictures of starvation and deprivation in Third World regions such as Biafra. 'Spend, spend, spend' could no longer be a justifiable credo when people were known to be dying of hunger. As a result, a widespread social conscience began to develop. Guilt bred introspection: at the individual level, psychoanalysis became popular in the hope that it would provide some answers.

Questioning brought with it rejection and protest. In the United States the hugely unpopular Vietnam War, which would drag on until 1975, was the cause of many student protests. In the United States's major cities dissatisfaction and frustration focused on social and political inequality and erupted into rioting in the black ghettos. Racial problems were further fuelled by the assassination of Martin Luther King in Memphis in 1968. In Paris, student riots erupted in the same year, and similar feelings of unrest and political frustration spread through much of Europe. Not surprisingly, the 1960s was a period of fierce nationalism, and the Stars and Stripes and the Union Jack were popular media and advertising images at this time.

However, protest was not always violent. The second half of the decade saw the emergence of the Hippies, people more concerned with peace and love, some of whom expressed their dislike for society by 'dropping out' altogether and living in self-sufficient communes. Others expressed their anti-war views through 'flower power': this form of protest included pop concerts and events, such as the much-publicized John Lennon and Yoko Ono lie-in, as well as putting flowers in the guns of soldiers being sent to war.

The outstanding technological achievement of the second half of the 1960s was the landing of Apollo 11 on the Moon in 1969. As J. F. Kennedy had promised in 1961, human beings were walking on the surface of another world before the decade was out. However, technological progress increasingly left in its wake all forms of waste which had traditionally been dumped on land tips or at sea. By the end of the 1960s, the effects of the wholesale consumerism of previous years could be seen in the many polluted areas of land, rivers and seas: the throw-away society had not catered for what would happen beyond the dustbin, and both domestic and industrial waste became a major problem for which no real means of disposal had yet been devised.

By the end of the 1960s most people in the industrialized countries had more choices than ever before. Health, education and housing were provided for most people, through either state or private schemes, and the booming retail trade offered a vast array of different products and makes from which to choose. Fashions and styles – no longer the prerogative of the wealthy – co-existed, and could be purchased in the high streets of the major towns and cities.

■ **Below** A male boutique in Carnaby Street, London, 1967. This shop was under the ownership of John Stephen, who ran nearly half of all the clothes shops in Carnaby Street at this time.

■ **Right** Under its Australian editor, Richard Neville, *Oz Magazine* carried not only 'underground' writing but also exciting illustrative material in startlingly bright colours.

Right Badges became a popular means of self-expression. Their messages concerned such matters as political persuasion and sexual preference.

Below On 31 July, 1969, astronauts Neil Armstrong and Buzz Aldrin walked on the surface of the moon. Their 'great leap for mankind' was watched by millions on live television.

Groovy Gear

The early 1960s had witnessed the ascendence of Britain as the source of inspiration for fashion design and retailing, but it was not long before the styles set on the streets and in the boutiques of London spread throughout Europe and all over the world. Young people, who had provided much of the original impetus, were now firmly established as a market force to be reckoned with: by 1967, 50 per cent of women's clothes manufactured in Britain were sold to people in the 15–19 years age group.

In response to the systematic rejection of fashion and clothing rules and conventions during the early 1960s, the second half of the decade witnessed extremes – hemlines reached unprecedented heights in the form of the 'micro' (1967), and true obsolescence materialized in the guise of the disposable paper dress (generally available from 1967). In addition, several designers introduced see-through clothing and in a few instances, such as in Rudi Gernreich's topless bathing costume, nudity was deemed acceptable (on the catwalks, at least) so long as the face was fully made-up.

The fashion houses of Paris took on board the relaxing of strict dress codes, but some of the clothes they produced were indelibly stamped with the visible signs of elitism; for example, Paco Rabanne's space-age chain-mail collection of 1966 was deliberately designed to look as expensive as it was. Designers such as Mary Quant and John Bates in Britain and Betsey Johnson in the United States continued to experiment with different fabrics and materials, including paper, nylon, plastics and elasticated fabrics.

Given the new technology and materials being applied to fashionable clothing, it was inevitable that a more romantic, natural style would begin to evolve. Vidal Sassoon's geometric haircut of 1966 was certainly severe, but it was also totally lacquer-free, relying on the natural shine of the hair for effect. Fashion photography of the period displayed a similar more naturalistic approach, with models laughing, running and having their hair blown about by the wind – all very different from the stiff poses of the previous decades.

The Hippy movement, which first surfaced in California (and from 1967 onward spread to the rest of the United States and then to other countries), nurtured a form of anti-fashion in which virtually all types of clothing were permissible, whether long or short, new or second-hand, patterned or plain, as long as the materials were natural. Despite a doctrine based on rejection of uniformity, a distinct style emerged, seeking inspiration from many sources, but utilizing military uniforms and 'ethnic' clothing in particular. The psychedelic imagery gleaned from the use of hallucinogenic drugs also affected clothes design, most notably in the exaggerated patterns and colours of fabrics that appeared at this time.

Throughout the 1960s, the distinctions between clothing made specifically for men and that made for women became generally less and less obvious. The trouser-suit for women had been launched in London and in Paris (by Courrèges) as early as 1964, and the early Mods had introduced the idea of colourful clothes for men. But it was the Hippy style of dressing that first introduced a totally unisex look: men and women wore their hair long and it was possible for both sexes to wear exactly the same clothes only in different sizes. Cotton 'loons' were unisex trousers that fitted neither sex properly, but at least they were cheap and available in a wide range of colours.

By the end of the decade it had become established that any number of different styles could co-exist, and fashions were no longer dictated by the centralized Paris couturiers. Such a climate encouraged an alarming appetite for different styles, and some clothes designers looked to the past for inspiration. Revivals of past styles became fashionable, the most notable of which were the Art Nouveau and Art Deco styles clearly seen in the clothes and graphics of Barbara Hulanicki's Biba store.

■ Right (inset) A Hippie, 1968. Torn and ripped clothes were no longer the prerogative of the homeless; middle-class youth scoured the secondhand stores in search of the desired degree of wear-and-tear.

Indian love-call.
By Christopher McDonnell.

Plain and plaid polyester / cotton woven by Galey & Lord — a division of Burlington Industries at Burlington House, New York, N.Y. 10019

■ Left Advertisement for Galey & Lord which appeared in *The New Yorker* in 1969. The loose shapes of Indian clothing (brought back to Europe and the United States by travelling Hippies) greatly influenced fashion design.

*I love
cool colours
with a sizzle*

Max Factor proves that cool lip colours are even more exciting when they sizzle a little. Peach Meringue . . . Crushed Coral . . . Petal Satin . . . Capistrano Pink . . . Tint of Pink . . . Strawberry Meringue . . . cool-cool lip colours that sizzle — enough to make anyone melt!

MAX FACTOR Lipstick Colours
...WITH TONING NAIL POLISH

Go Dotty this Spring

Dorothy Gray's
new lipstick colours
are the wildest yet!

DOTTY PINK! A madly-love-you blush of a pink.
DOTTY ORANGE! A hot dotty zing of a tint.

They're the dottiest colours yet — beware! See them more and glowing on your lips. Try them, for fun, with LIGHTS UP YELLOW — the lipstick that gives exciting new tints to any colour!

And with your new dotty lipstick, have a new dotty compact—filled with Sheer Elation pressed powder, hint of Portrait Foundation and the wild-eyed make-up. Go on, Go dotty!

Have a fling—it's Spring!

DOROTHY GRAY
NEW YORK, LONDON, PARIS
45 CONDUIT STREET, LONDON, W.1, REGENT 2704

■ Two advertisements for
different brands of cosmetics,
illustrating the colourful clothing
sold to both women and men
during this period. One (**above**)
uses sexual voyeurism to sell the
product, while the other (**left**)
makes reference to the
hallucinogenic experience.

Furnishing the Pad

The first signs of Pop culture influencing furniture design could have been seen in the early 1960s, but it took several years for the stylistic themes to penetrate the popular markets. Primary colours, bold designs and undiluted geometric shapes began to be applied to furniture and furnishing fabrics alike, although it was not until the end of the decade that such items of furniture were available from less-exclusive outlets and at an affordable price. Knock-down furniture, stimulated by the growth in popularity of DIY (do it yourself), was widely available from 1965 onwards and became a cheap way for people to buy new designs.

It was not only Pop imagery that was applied to furniture: the Pop mentality was equally applicable. Furniture began to be produced that redefined the ground rules – for example, cardboard chairs to throw away after a couple of months and 'bean bags' that depended on the sitter to define the shape of the chair. In extreme cases living-room furniture could be abandoned altogether, to be replaced by giant cushions on the floor.

Much of the innovation in design was dependent on the use of new or improved materials, particularly plastics. Plastic had already entered the mainstream of furniture design, most notably in the form of moulded plastic chairs for offices and dining rooms, but with the advent of inflatable chairs it could be used overtly in living rooms. The first manufactured blow-up model to achieve international notoriety was one designed by Paolo Lomazzi, Donato d'Urbino and Jonathan de Pas for Zanotta in 1967, although inflatable furniture was available in Denmark as early as 1961. It certainly had its advantages, in so far as it could be produced in any number of colours and could be stored away when not in use. However, for heavy smokers and those not so keen on keeping up the repairs, these chairs were less appealing.

Zanotta were responsible also for producing the 'Sacco' chair, designed by Piero Gatti, Cesare Paolini and Franco Teodoro in 1969 (although prototypes had been made several years earlier). This chair consisted of a large sealed fabric bag containing a filling consisting of millions of tiny polystyrene balls which moulded to the shape of the body.

At the further extremes of 1960s furniture were the surreal pieces, heavily influenced by the Pop sculpture of Claes Oldenburg. Jon Wealleans and Jon Wright produced a chair that resembled a huge set of teeth, and in 1969 Allen Jones produced a chair, table and coat-stand in the forms of women distorting themselves in accordance with a festishist's dream.

The Pad

The majority of homes in the 1960s were furnished with an eclectic mixture of furniture from a variety of periods, but the increase in the numbers of young people setting up home in their own flats and bedsits bred a new, 'young' environment. This style was often dependent on large, bold images, such as posters and brightly coloured bedspreads and window blinds set off against coloured walls. Finishing touches included old advertising signs, the obligatory record player blaring out pop music and 'joss sticks' scenting the air. The use of tinfoil as wallpaper at this time reflected the influence of the 'space race', and was also handy for the indoor cultivation of marijuana plants – a popular pastime among Hippies (and the Radical Chic). Above all, the style reflected the heightened awareness of the senses, influenced by Hippy and drug culture. Theatricality was all-important, and it was during this period that spotlights began to be used in domestic interiors. Before long, many of the ideas generated by the young were easing their way into adult markets and interiors.

■ **Above** An advertisement for bedspread and towels which featured in *The New Yorker* in 1969. Bold geometric shapes in bright colours were popular motifs for furnishing fabrics.

■ **Above** A capsule kitchen on show at the Design Centre in 1968. This style was made possible by the advent of moulded synthetic materials.

■ **Below** A double rocker designed in 1967 by Donald Goodship – one of the more fanciful pieces of furniture on sale at this time.

■ **Right** 'Sacco' chair designed by Piero Gatti, Cesare Paolini and Franco Teodoro, and put into production by Zanotta in 1969.

Status Styling

Production of consumer goods steadily rose throughout the 1960s, meeting and creating demand, and leaving obsolete models in its wake. In some cases, genuinely new products did become available, such as the nonstick frying pan (a spin-off from NASA's spacecraft technology), but in many cases so-called new products were just existing products altered in design as a result of the impact of new technology. The developments in the uses of moulded plastics and nylon meant that the structure and casing of many products altered drastically, often completely changing the style of the product in the process.

A factor behind the greater demand for household goods was the growing number of young people setting up home on their own and needing a full new set of products. More important, however, was the 'disposable' income that a greater number of people had available to spend on consumer or 'luxury' goods. In addition, manufacturers were quick to realize that, if they brought out a new and slightly different model each year, the consumer was likely to buy it, thereby dictating to – as well as responding to – the market. The styling of products to reflect shifts in fashion was, therefore, vital for the maintenance of sales.

Throughout the 1960s Japan and the Far East continued to export goods to the United States and Europe. Traditionally, their products had been considered unstylish but correspondingly cheap, their poor designs being based directly on Western ideas. However, some of the major firms, such as Sony – who had established a design department in the 1950s – began to concentrate on a more acceptable appearance to their products, and by the 1960s these firms were beginning to show results: not only were their goods technically sound, they also looked good. From 1965 onward, Japanese cars began to sell internationally in large quantities, pioneered by the Toyota Corona, the first Japanese car to fully penetrate the notoriously difficult US market. Interestingly enough, the imports of foreign goods into Britain produced a series of patriotic campaigns, the most publicized of which was the 'I'm Backing Britain' campaign of 1967. At Expo '67, an international fair held in Montreal, the British stand focused on a Mini painted with the Union Jack.

In the field of office equipment and design, Olivetti's technological advances included the introduction of their first desk-top computer, designed by Mario Bellini and produced in 1966. Olivetti's concern with improving the office working environment (reflecting a generally felt humanitarian approach to working conditions) resulted in the 'Sistema 45' range of office furniture, designed by Ettore Sottsass and produced in 1969. It incorporated strong colours and rounded, less aggressive shapes all coordinated into a unified system. Another product to come under Sottsass' scrutiny (together with Perry King) was the typewriter. In 1969 Olivetti brought out the 'Valentine' typewriter, which was encased in a bright red body. Working could be fun, too.

■ **Below** A Braun shaver manufactured in 1969. Cased in stainless steel, the shaver bears all the slick styling characteristic of the company.

Left The Valentine portable typewriter designed by Ettore Sottsass with Perry King and put into production by Olivetti in 1969.

Above (inset) A magazine advertisement for the Ford Thunderbird. The device of using sexy women to sell cars to men was used increasingly in the 1960s.

Left (inset) As interior design began to incorporate bright colours, so consumer products had to follow suit. This Murphy television, introduced in 1967, was available in eight different colours.

Here Today ...

■ Pop culture demanded instant gratification; staying power was not a prerequisite for a successful product. As a result, many of the items which came on the market were designed to last only as long as the customer's interest. Peter Murdoch's cardboard chair for children (1964) (**below**) was one; although designed in Britain it was manufactured in the United States.

■ Other products were designed to be used once and then thrown away. These included canned soft drinks (**above**), magazines (**right**) and paper cups and plates (**left**). However, the mass production of disposable products created an equal amount of waste material, much of which turned up on the beaches.

Over the Moon

■ The depiction of space and spacemen during the 1950s had been closer to science fiction than science fact. However, in the 1960s, when men were not only floating in space but actually walking on the surface of the Moon, the 'right stuff' was readily available.

■ The inspiration behind Eddie Squire's 1969 fabric design, *Lunar Rocket* (**inset left**), is all too apparent. Shown (**left**) is the launch of *Apollo II* in the same year. Again from 1969 was Sue Palmer's *Space Walk* fabric design (**inset right**) with its source of inspiration equally obvious. These silver-suited astronauts (**right**) were the first team selected by the National Aeronautics and Space Administration (NASA) for their *Mercury* programme.

Looking to the Past:
Nostalgia and Revivalism

The quickening pace of modernization throughout the 1950s and 1960s brought with it a nostalgia for the past as well as a reappraisal of rural ideals. A belief that 'real' and lasting values were in danger of being swept away by permissiveness and technological achievement was deeply felt. Terence Conran's Habitat store, opened in 1964, recognized this yearning. It stocked not only contemporary designs but also crafted furniture and kitchen equipment made from intrinsically beautiful natural materials, such as wood and marble, that appeared to come from a French farmhouse kitchen rather than from a designer's drawing board.

This reappearance of 'traditional' designs fostered a growing interest in ephemera – such as old enamel advertising signs and grocery packets, originals and reproductions of which were available from Dodo Designs off the Portobello Road. Similarly, antique and second-hand clothing became acceptable – for example, old military uniforms and top hats. The cover of the Beatles' *Sgt. Pepper's Lonely Hearts Club Band*, designed by Peter Blake, not only featured Edwardian-inspired clothing, its overall design owed much to old music-hall imagery.

The adoption of retrospective and nostalgic designs was a strong theme in the second half of the 1960s and the early 1970s. The main decorative styles that were exploited for inspiration during the 1960s were Art Nouveau and Art Deco. Whether the attitude of 'looking to the past' was in response to the ravenous appetite of Pop culture for 'fresh' ideas, or whether it was a heartfelt yearning for past standards and values in the light of increasing modernization, 'retro' became wide-

■ **Right** The cover of *Sgt Pepper's Lonely Hearts Club Band,* designed in 1967 by Peter Blake in collaboration with his wife Jan Haworth and the photographer Michael Cooper. The typography on the drum and the theatrical uniforms are based on turn-of-the-century models.

RAZZ-A-MA-TAZZ
(says our 1968/Thirties girl)

Make-up created by David and Eric Aylott.

Eylure make your eyes say beautiful things

She's got Eylure! That's why her eyes shine out at you: alluring, romantic, terrific, divine! All the thirties words you can think of only more so. Because our 1968/Thirties Girl has a lot more going for her than any girl had way back in the Thirties.
She's got Eylure—lustrous sable ** lashes and

individual under-lashes; Eylure mascara; soft, smoky Eylure Shado-matte, Eylure brow pencil —and a subtle beauty spot.
How do you get Eylure? There are more than twenty different kinds of lashes to choose from. And you can actually try them at your nearest Trylash Bar in leading shops and chemists.

For more details of the Thirties Look, write to Miss Treena Price, Dept SC, 8 Grosvenor Street, London W1

EYLURE

■ **Above** 1920s and 1930s styling came back into vogue from 1966 onwards. This advertisement for false eyelashes draws heavily on a 1930s 'Hollywood' look.

■ **Right** 1960s nostalgia in Britain focused on 'the days of the Empire' and the Union Jack. Whether sold on London's Portobello Road or used by the government to encourage nationalism, as here, the Union Jack featured prominently during the second half of the 1960s.

spread, particularly in graphic and interior design.

The reawakening of interest in the Art Nouveau style can be detected as early as 1960, when a large retrospective exhibition was held at the Museum of Modern Art, New York. Other influential events included an Alphonse Mucha exhibition (1963) and an Aubrey Beardsley exhibition (1966), both staged at the Victoria and Albert Museum, London. Inspiration came also from the movies – Cecil Beaton's costumes for *My Fair Lady* (1964) being a notable example – and from many books that were published at this time. It seemed fitting that the 'Swinging Sixties' should seek inspiration from the 'Naughty Nineties'. Barbara Hulanicki adopted the style wholesale, using pieces of period furniture to furnish her store, Biba, when it opened in 1964, and Art-Nouveau-inspired graphics to market it.

Art Deco was the natural successor to Art Nouveau retro, and its impact lasted well into the 1970s. Like its predecessor, it was brought to most people's attention by a large retrospective exhibition – this one was held in Paris in 1966 and called *Les Années: Les Arts Deco* (where the commonly used term comes from) – and by many magazine articles that appeared around the world. Imagery from movies such as *Bonnie and Clyde* (1967) and *Thoroughly Modern Millie* (1967) likewise helped to awaken public interest in the style. Furniture design was less affected, but the graphic images of the 1960s – posters, record covers, and so on – display a plethora of Art Deco typography and styling.

I'M BACKING BRITAIN

Psychedelia

The 'mind-blowing' style that emerged in the latter half of the 1960s was psychedelia. Cultivated in the deeper recesses of the mind, often with the help of hallucinogenic drugs, the style at its height pervaded the more conscious areas of human existence – clothes, music and particularly graphics. The most noticeable visual signs of the style were swirling shapes and luminous colours. Many graphic designs gave the impression that the newly revived patterns of Art Nouveau had been spun slowly in a washing machine with a good dose of colour enhancer.

The style undoubtedly had its roots in the drug culture that had been gaining ground throughout the 1960s. The Mods had used amphetamines from the beginning of the decade, and marijuana gradually became available through 'dealers', but it was lysergic acid diethylamide (LSD), with its hallucinogenic properties, that provided the mental and visual stimulus behind psychedelia. In the United States, Dr Timothy Leary championed the drug and got mass-media coverage for his efforts. His message – 'Turn on, tune in, drop out' – was heard loud and clear, from San Francisco to Vietnam. The search for solutions within the subconscious revealed a denial of, or at least dissatisfaction with, the conscious environment and all the materialistic, commercial elements that went with it.

Bands (the term 'pop group' had become derogatory) such as Jefferson Airplane, the Soft Machine and the Grateful Dead produced LPs of lengthy, sometimes purely instrumental compositions, some of which were deliberately distorted in the recording studios to help evoke the hallucinatory experience. From 1966 onward the Beatles produced several songs with thinly disguised references to drugs, including 'Lucy in the Sky with Diamonds' from their 1967 album, *Sgt. Pepper's Lonely Hearts Club Band*.

The origin of the graphic psychedelic style is often traced to Wes Wilson, who produced some striking poster designs for concerts at the Fillmore Auditorium, California. In Britain, Michael English and Nigel Weymouth formed a partnership called 'Hapshash and the Coloured Coat' and produced many psychedelic and surreal posters, record jackets and murals, including a giant Red Indian face for the façade of the 'Granny Takes a Trip' store in 1967. *Oz* magazine, published in London under the editorship of the Australian Richard Neville, published psychedelic graphics and imagery, particularly the work of fellow-Australian Martin Sharp, perhaps most famous for his psychedelic rendering of Jimi Hendrix.

Psychedelic patterns and colours quickly found their way onto mass-produced fabrics and clothes, and even penetrated corporate design when Alexander Calder covered one of Braniff International's aircraft with coloured swirls. However, the style was so strong and so unsympathetic to other styles that it was inevitable that psychedelia departed as quickly as it had arrived. As early as the start of 1968 there were already complaints of 'overdose'.

■ **Below** Jimi Hendrix.

■ **Right** The bright colours and swirling shapes of psychedelic patterns were meant to be influenced by the hallucinations experienced by people 'tripping' on drugs such as LSD.

■ **Right (inset)** Advertisement for a bank, 1968. Deliberately confusing images, often created using projectors, were a common psychedelic device.

■ **Below** Invitation to a discotheque, *c.* 1968. The development and use of synthetic dyes enabled bright 'day-glo' colours to be used for printing.

How can we help you make the scene a brighter prospect still?

DISTRICT BANK

This is a ticket for two to see 'HAIR' DISCOTHEQUE

Visual Anarchy

Psychedelia was largely a product of California's Hippy movement. Its graphics usually comprised a dense collage of day-glo coloured images such as flowers, faces and rainbows. It soon found its way into the art of posters and record covers, good examples of the latter being Martin Sharp's cover for the *Disraeli Gears* (1967) album by Cream, and Michael Cooper's design for the Rolling Stones' *Their Satanic Majesties Request* (also 1967).

The psychedelic era spawned its own magazines. *International Times*, first published in 1966, and *Oz*, launched the following year, both catered to the idealistic, anti-establishment counter-culture that was emerging in Britain. *Oz* was renowned for its anarchic visual style, in which pictures were often out of focus or superimposed, and type was laid diagonally or even upside-down. Between 1967 and 1970 the controversial British 'New Wave' science-fiction magazine *New Worlds* used similar graphic techniques to great effect, although with a little more restraint.

In the wider magazine world, the escalating cost of production hit the large-format picture titles hard, as did competition from television, and in the United States both *Look* and *Life* were closed down. The growing public concern with social issues such as the Vietnam War contributed to the success of more serious magazines like *Time* and *Newsweek*. In West Germany, the magazine *Twen* established a reputation for the strong visual impact of its layout.

■ **Above** The simple-coloured flowers of this advertisement for Cat Girl Tights are reminiscent of the 'daisy' graphic used by fashion designer Mary Quant.

■ **Left** *International Times* was one of the visually anarchic, anti-establishment magazines spawned by the counter culture of the late 1960s.

■ **Above right** The logo for the Biba fashion store in London provides a fine example of the revival of the Art Nouveau style in graphics.

■ **Right** *Nova* was one of the most visually inventive magazines of the 1960s. Its pilot issue boasted: 'A new kind of magazine for the new kind of woman'.

In advertising, the late 1960s was a time of great slogans – 'Beanz Meanz Heinz', Esso's (Exxon's) 'Put a Tiger in Your Tank' and 'High Speed Gas'. Even the British Government became interested in a more creative style of advertising: a striking newspaper ad showing the tar collected in a smoker's lungs was produced for the Health Education Council by a young Charles Saatchi.

In the field of corporate identity, one of the most important designs of the decade was a new logo for the Mobil Oil company, designed in 1966 by the company Chermayeff and Geismar. In Europe, the designer F. K. H. Henrion created new corporate identities for two airlines, the Dutch carrier KLM in 1964 and BEA four years later in 1968.

The 1960s was an important decade for public information design. A system of road signs had long before been introduced in Britain; in 1965 the Design Research Unit produced a similar system for British Rail. Information design found a role at the 1968 Olympic Games in Mexico, too. Here a vast and comprehensive array of pictographic signs based upon the host country's traditional Aztec and folk art was designed by an international team.

One final area in which there was a burst of graphic creativity in the late 1960s was British stamp design. With the active encouragement of Postmaster General Anthony Wedgwood Benn (today known simply as Tony Benn), a series of colourful designs was commissioned around topical subjects like the 900th anniversary of the Battle of Hastings, England's World Cup soccer victory in 1966, and the opening of London's Post Office Tower.

Cementing the Style

The 1960s saw the departure of the great pioneers of the Modern movement: Frank Lloyd Wright had died in 1959, Le Corbusier died in 1965, and Mies van de Rohe gave up the practice of architecture in 1967. The spirit of the movement, however, lived on in a second generation of architects – although their efforts to develop wider personal vocabularies were generally regarded by the old guard as a betrayal of principles. Three architects from widely different parts of the world are representative of this second generation: John Utzon, Louis Kahn and Kenzo Tange.

Utzon had only a small practice in Denmark when in 1957 he won the international competition to design the Sydney Opera House. The building was completed in 1973 – long after Utzon's retirement and in acrimonious circumstances. This spectacular building consists of two principal elements; a solid rock-like base containing ancillary areas and a great superstructure of shining tile-covered shells soaring above it, enveloping the two major halls. The base, surfaced with reconstructed granite, rises in massive steps to the halls, whose dished floors are pressed into the base like great thumbprints. The drama of the structure dominates all – both externally and internally – the great shells springing and fanning out from massive point supports. The functions of the building take place within the spaces left by the structure.

The second architect, Louis Kahn, developed a very personal vocabulary of ordered formality. Its characteristics were the use of simple geometric forms, such as the cube and the cylinder, and the interplay of large geometrical openings in solid load-bearing walls of brick or concrete. His plans, too, make emphatic use of geometry, in particular of the square within the circle and the circle within the square. In Kahn's Assembly Building for the new capital of East Pakistan (now Bangladesh) at Dacca, commissioned in 1962, no frame or light structure interrupts the simple, solid forms defined by the load-bearing walls. No roof or eaves appear above the parapets to challenge the dominance of the walls. Doors, windows, railings and all minor elements are played down, giving the building strength from its simplicity.

Kenzo Tange was commissioned to design two arenas for the 1964 Tokyo Olympics. The larger of the two, the swimming pool, has something in common with Utzon's opera house. It is an enormous structure – seating over 16,000 people – and it is a showpiece of national prestige, taking contemporary building technology to the limits. A great concrete saucer of stepped seating forms a base and an anchor. Two concrete masts at either end of the arena support a pair of massive parallel cables in tension, as in a suspension bridge, and from these hangs a tent of welded steel plates on a steel net. The catenary curves of the cables and tent are reflected in the curves of the plan to produce an interior like the belly of Jonah's whale.

Also of great significance during the 1960s was the production of 'visionary' architecture – plans and drawings that were usually the blueprints for unbuildable structures. The main exponents of this practice were a group of architects working together under the title Archigram. Their influence was deep-felt, particularly in Italy where Archizoom followed a similar way of working.

■ **Right** The Sydney Opera House, designed by John Utzon and completed in 1973. The building was a brave architectural statement, but one that paid off.

■ **Below** National Assembly building at Dacca, Bangladesh, designed by the US architect Louis Kahn. Building began in 1962 and took 12 years to complete.

Right Gymnasium complex in Tokyo, designed by Kenzo Tange and completed in 1964.

Above (inset) Inside the main swimming pool arena of the Tokyo gymnasium. The huge roof is supported by steel cables stretched between the two supporting pillars.

'To the barricades!'

Violent protests in the 1960s can be divided into two main categories: those provoked by racial tensions, such as the ghetto riots in the United States, and those arising from the revolutionary ideals and fears of the 'New Left', such as the student riots in Paris and the worldwide protests against the Vietnam War and general US 'imperialism'.

The riots in the black ghettos of US cities in the 1960s were directly descended from the peaceful protest movements of the 1950s. Protesters in the 1950s fought against segregation and for equal rights by, for example, staging bus boycotts, and they publicized their cause through long marches – many whites took part. By the early 1960s the most popular form of protest was the sit-in. Despite the passing of the Civil Rights Bill by the Senate in 1960, many blacks were still unhappy at the slow rate of change and the conditions in which they had to live. The growth of the suburbs in the 1950s had meant that well off whites had moved out of inner cities, leaving them to become ghettos inhabited only by poor blacks. Dissatisfaction erupted in violence in the summer of 1964, when New York blacks rioted in Harlem and Bedford-Stuyvesant. By the end of the 1960s, more than 300 US cities – notably Chicago and Detroit – had experienced racially motivated black group violence. 1967 was the most violent year: 71 major riots took place. The assassination of Martin Luther King in 1968 sparked off a series of riots affecting 100 cities.

Black militancy was seen also in the rise of such groups as the Black Muslims and Black Panthers. The emergence of these organizations was a result of the apparent failure of the civil-rights laws and of peaceful protest. One of the most famous proponents of direct action, Malcolm X, said: 'The day of non-violent resistance is over.' The slogan of these groups was 'Black Power' and they preached black pride – emphasizing the African roots of US blacks.

Yet, while the ghetto riots and 'Black Power' movements were predominantly US phenomena, the rise of the 'New Left' was international. The phrase 'New Left' can be used to describe various disparate groups of the 1960s which tended to be united by their rejection of traditional party politics and their belief in direct action. They were also very anti-American, believing that the United States (particularly in Vietnam) was operating a kind of imperialism. Protests against US involvement in Vietnam took place all over the world, with protesters in the United States burning their draft cards in public and staging demonstrations outside the Pentagon. The anti-American feeling was particularly strong in Japan, where many people resented the presence of US bases. Japanese students tended to be very militant and reacted violently to the US presence and to their own country's authoritarianism.

In fact, students were at the forefront of the 'New Left' movement – revering revolutionaries such as North Vietnam's Ho Chi Minh, Russia's V.I. Lenin and the Cuban rebel Che Guevara. And it was students who were behind the most notable protests of the decade – which took place in Paris over May and June 1968 and were echoed in Britain and Germany. The Paris 'student-worker revolution' started when police violently broke up student demonstrations at the University of Paris (the Sorbonne). With the help of many ordinary Parisians, students took over the city's Latin Quarter, erecting barricades against the police, and sympathetic workers occupied factories. Despite the strength of feelings surrounding the Paris revolt – intensified by police violence – it succeeded only in showing up the weaknesses of the Gaullist regime, leading to the resignation of President de Gaulle himself in 1969. Nevertheless, it represented the high point of 'New Left' action in the 1960s; never since then have workers and students united so willingly.

■ **Right** Paris, France, 1968. In the most notable protest of the decade, workers and students united against the police, erecting barricades and occupying factories.

■ **Left** Malcolm X: 'The day of non-violent resistance is over.'

■ **Right** The assassination of Martin Luther King in 1968 sparked off a series of riots in which the National Guard were mobilized to stop looting.

■ **Far right** The United States' involvement in the Vietnam War brought protesters to the streets all over the world. Here a peace demonstrator taunts the MPs outside the Pentagon.

Peaceful Protest

■ The Campaign for Nuclear Disarmament's symbol (**above**) and the victory sign (**right**) – formerly associated with war – became synonymous with peace.

Left Bob Dylan, the voice of a generation.

Below Psychedelia and desert boots around the campfire.

Bottom The belief that love, music and simple living could produce a political change reached its apotheosis in Woodstock – the largest gathering of young people this century.

'50s and '60s Chronology

YEAR	UNITED STATES	UNITED KINGDOM
50		● *Mediterranean Food*, Elizabeth David
51		● Festival of Britain ● Comet I launched ● New Conservative Government (Churchill P.M.) ● Burgess & Maclean defect to Soviet Union
52	● US explodes first hydrogen bomb ● 'Wire' chair, Harry Bertoia ● Eisenhower president	● Accession of Queen Elizabeth II
53		● Queen Elizabeth II crowned
54	● *The Wild Ones* ● US troops to Vietnam	● *Lucky Jim*, Kingsley Amis
55	● Boeing 707 launched ● *Rock Around the Clock* ● *Rebel Without a Cause* ● *Monogram*, Robert Rauschenberg (completed 1959)	● Commercial TV launched ● Mary Quant's Bazaar opens
56	● Lounge chair, Charles Eames ● *Heartbreak Hotel*, Elvis Presley	● Design Centre opens ● *Just What Is It That Makes Today's Homes So Different, So Appealing?*, Richard Hamilton ● First nuclear power station opened ● *Look Back in Anger*, John Osborne
57	● *On the Road*, Jack Kerouac ● Cadillac Eldorado	
58	● Seagram Building completed	● Race riots in London
59	● Guggenheim Museum opened	● Austin Mini Minor launched ● M1 motorway opened
60	● *Moments Preserved*, Irving Penn ● The 'Pill' introduced ● Civil Rights Bill	● *The Caretaker*, Harold Pinter
61	● *Breakfast at Tiffany's*	● E-Type Jaguar launched ● Commonwealth Immigration Bill ● Archigram started
62	● *Marilyn Monroe Diptych*, Andy Warhol	● Polypropylene chair, Robin Day ● Coventry Cathedral completed
63	● J. F. Kennedy assassinated ● IBM System 360	● *Fall*, Bridget Riley ● Profumo affair
64	● *As I Opened Fire*, Roy Lichtenstein	● Habitat opens ● Biba started ● New Labour Government (Wilson P.M.)
65		● Death of Sir Winston Churchill
66	● Mirrored Room, Lucas Samaras	● England wins World Cup
67	● *Barbarella* ● Apollo II reaches Moon	● *A Bigger Splash*, David Hockney ● *Sgt. Pepper's Lonely Hearts Club Band* ● *Blow Up*
68	● M. L. King assassinated ● Ghetto riots	● *2001 – A Space Odyssey* ● Grosvenor Square riots
69	● *Easy Rider* ● Armstrong and Aldrin walk on the Moon	● Mr Freedom opens ● 'Fetish' furniture, Allen Jones

E U R O P E	OTHER COUNTRIES	YEAR
● 'Tubino' light	● Outbreak of Korean War (ends 1953) ● 'Hunting' chair, Børge Hogensen	**50**
● Milan Triennale ● Rat für Formgebung established, Germany ● 550 shaver, Braun	● Soviet Union explodes atomic bomb	**51**
	● Japanese Industrial Designers' Association formed	**52**
● 'Stile Industria' launched, Italy	● Death of Stalin ● Soviet Union explodes hydrogen bomb ● Mount Everest conquered	**53**
● Milan Triennale	● *The Seven Samurai* ● Nasser comes to power, Egypt	**54**
● Hochschule für Gestaltung, Germany	● TR-55 radio, Sony (TTK)	**55**
● Soviet Union invades Hungary	● Suez Crisis	**56**
● Milan Triennale ● Mirella sewing machine, Marcello Nizzoli ● Common Market formed - Treaty of Rome ● *Mythologies*, Roland Barthes ● Fiat '500' launched ● Citröen DS19 launched	● Sputnik 1 launched ● Syndey Opera House begun (completed 1973)	**57**
● De Gaulle president, France ● 'Egg' chair, Arne Jacobsen ● Brussels World Fair	● *Dr Zhivago*, Boris Pasternak ● Nikita Khruschev comes to power, Soviet Union	**58**
● *La Dolce Vita* ● Chanel suit	● Castro in power, Cuba ● TV-8-301 Portable mini TV, Sony	**59**
● *Jules et Jim*, Trouffaut		**60**
	● Yuri Gagarin first man in space	**61**
● 'Arco' light, Achilles Castiglione		**62**
● *Les Mots*, Jean-Paul Sartre	● Tokkaido train launched	**63**
● Space Age collection, Courréges	● Tokyo olympic arena completed	**64**
● Space Age collection, Ungaro ● *Alphaville*, Godard	● 'Hammond' chair, Poul Kjaerholm	**65**
● 'Globe' chair, Eero Aarnio ● Archizoom established, Italy		**66**
● Inflatable chair, De Pas, D'Urbino and Lomazzi	● Expo '67, Montreal	**67**
● 'Sacco' chair, Zanotta ● Paris student riots	● Soviet Union invades Czechoslovakia	**68**
● 'Valentine' typewriter, Olivetti		**69**

Select Bibliography

Anderson Black, J., Garland, Madge, and Kennett, Frances, *A History of Fashion*, Orbis Publishing, 1983

Banham, Mary and Hillier, Bevis, *A Tonic to the Nation*, Thames & Hudson, 1976

Banham, Reyner, (Ed. Penny Sparke), *Design by Choice*, Rizzoli, 1981

Bayer, William, *The Great Movies*, Hamlyn Publishing, 1978

Bayley, Stephen, *The Conran Directory of Design*, Conran Octopus, 1985

Bayley, Stephen, Garner, Philippe, and Sudjic, Deyan, *Twentieth-Century Style and Design*, Thames & Hudson, 1986

Brodie, Douglas, *The Films of the Fifties*, Citadel Press, 1976

Brodie, Douglas, *The Films of the Sixties*, Citadel Press, 1980

Carter, Ernestine, *20th Century Fashion – A Scrapbook 1900 to Today*, Eyre Methuen, 1975

Cowie, Peter (Ed.), *A Concise History of the Cinema*, Vol 2, A. S. Barnes, 1971

Dorner, Jane, *Fashion in the Forties and Fifties*, Ian Allen, 1975

Feagin, Joe R., and Hahn, Warlan, *Ghetto Revolts, The Politics of Violence in American Cities*, Macmillan Publishing Co., 1973

Forty, Adrian, *Objects of Desire*, Thames & Hudson, 1986

Garner, Philippe, *Contemporary Decorative Arts*, Chartwell, 1980

Glynn, Prudence, with Ginsburg, Madelaine, *In Fashion. Dress in the Twentieth Century*, George Allen & Unwin, 1979

Harker, Dave, *One for the Money. Politics and Popular Song*, Hutchinson, 1980

Harris, Jennifer, Hyde, Sarah, and Smith, Greg, *1966 and All That*, Trefoil, 1986

Harris, Nathaniel, *The Sixties. An Illustrated History 1960-1970*, Macdonald Educational, 1984

Hatje, Gerd and Ursula, *Design for Modern Living*, Thames & Hudson, 1962

Hebdige, Dick, *Subculture and the Meaning of Style*, Methuen, 1979

Heskett, John, *Industrial Design*, Oxford University Press, 1980

Hiesinger, Kathryn B., and Marcus, George H. (Eds.), *Design Since 1945*, Thames & Hudson, 1983

Hillier, Bevis, *The Style of the Century*, E. P. Dutton, 1983

Hine, Thomas, *Populux*, Alfred A. Knopf, 1986

Horn, Richard, *Fifties Style. Then and Now*, Columbus Books, 1985

Katz, Sylvia, *Classic Plastics From Bakelite to High-Tech*, Thames & Hudson, 1984

Lake, Frances, (Ed.), *Daily Mail Ideal Home Book 1953-4*, Daily Mail Ideal Home Publication, 1954

Lucie-Smith, Edward, *Cultural Calendar of the 20th Century*, Phaidon, 1979

Lucie-Smith, Edward, *A History of British Design*, Phaidon Press, 1983

Lucie-Smith, Edward, *Movements in Arts Since 1945*, (World of Art), Thames & Hudson, 1984

MacCarthy, Fiona, *A History of British Design 1830-1970*, Herbert Press, 1983

Mast, Gerald, *A Short History of the Movies*, Oxford University Press, 1982

Mayne, Richard, *Post War. The Dawn of Today's Europe*, Thames & Hudson, 1983

Opie, Robert, *Rule Britannia*, Viking, 1985

Robinson, David, (Cons. Ed.), and Lloyd, Ann (Ed.), *An Illustrated History of the Cinema*, Orbis Publishing, 1986

Sherman, Margaret (Ed.), *Daily Mail Ideal Home Book 1951-2*, Daily Mail Ideal Home Publication, 1952

Shipman, David, *The Story of the Cinema Vol. 2. From 'Citizen Cane' to the Present Day*, Hodder & Stoughton, 1984

Sissons, Michael, and French, Philip (Eds.), *Age of Austerity*, Oxford University Press, 1986

Sparke, Penny, Hodges, Felice, Stone, Anne, and Dent Coad, Emma, *Design Source Book*, Chartwell, 1986

Sparke, Penny, *An Introduction to Design and Culture in the Twentieth Century*, Allen & Unwin, 1986

Stavenow, Ake, and Huldt, Ake H. (Eds.), *Design in Sweden*, Gothia, 1961

Whiteley, Nigel, *Pop Design*, Design Council Publications, 1986

Picture Credits

The authors and publishers have made every effort to identify the copyright owners of the pictures used in this book; they apologize for any omissions and would like to thank the following:

Key: *l*=left; *r*=right; *t*=top; *b*=bottom; *c*=centre; *i*=inset; *m*=main picture.

Architectural Association: pages 34, 35 *t*, 55 *br*, 116. Arteluce: page 64 *b*. Austin Rover: page 60. Australian Overseas Information Services, London: page 117 *t*. BBC Hulton Picture Library: pages 8, 10, 11 *b*, 14 *r*, 15 *t*, 18 *t*, 19 *b*, 40 *b*, 43 *il*, 45 *m*, 49 *tr b*, 51 *br*, 74, 75 *tr b*, 81 *tl*, 94 *i*, 98, 101 *i*, 119 *t*, 121 *tr*. Boeing Commercial Aircraft Company: page 66. Braun: pages 26 *t*, 37 *tr*, 104. Bridgeman Art Library: pages 51 *t*, 82 *b* (© Bridget Riley), 83 *i* (© DACS 1982). Chanel: page 61 *b*. The Design Council Picture Library: pages 18 *b*, 20 *t*, 24 *t*, 25 *b*, 42 *i*, 53, 59, 64 *t*, 80, 87 *bl br*, 89-90, 91 *tl b*, 103 *t bl*, 106 *tl b*, 108 *i*, 109 *i*, 115 *t*. Christian Dior: pages 30 *b*, 31. Domus: page 103 *br*. EMI Records: page 110. Flos: page 64 *c*. Ford USA: page 67 *b i*. Solomon R Guggenheim Museum, New York: pages 38 (photo. Carmello Guadagno), 54 (photo. David Heald). Heals Archives: page 52 *tr br*. Hoover Ltd: 28 *b*. IBM UK Ltd: page 88 *b*. Illustrated London News: page 33 *bl*. Japan Information Centre: page 117 *b i*. Dan Johnston: page 65 *i*. Keystone Collection: pages 43 *ir*, 78. Kobal Collection Ltd: pages 79 *m*, 92 *b* (Paramount), 93 *t* (British Lion Films). Lionel Martinez: page 120. Movie Star News, New York: pages 33 *br*, 36, 42 *m*, 43 *m*, 44, 46 *b*, 47, 62, 63 *l*, 76 *l r*, 92 *t*, 93 *b*, 112, 121 *tl b*. NASA: pages 72 *t*, 99 *b*, 108 *m*, 109 *m*. The Observer Magazine: page 87 *t*, 99 *tr*. Olivetti: pages 26 *b*, 105 *m*. The Robert Opie Collection: pages 14 *l*, 17 *t bl br*, 19 *t i*, 20 *b*, 21, 22-3, 24 *b*, 25 *t*, 28 *t*, 29, 32, 33 *t*, 35 *bl br*, 37 *tl b*, 45 *it*, 46 *t*, 50, 51 *bl*, 56, 57, 58 *tr cr br*, 61 *tr*, 63 *t*, 65 *m*, 67 *t*, 68-70, 73 *t*, 75 *tl*, 76 *il ir*, 77, 79 *il ir*, 81 *tr*, 82 *t*, 84, 85 *r*, 91 *tr*, 94 *m*, 95 *i*, 96, 99 *tl*, 100, 101 *t b*, 102, 105 *it ib*, 106 *tr*, 107, 111, 113-4, 115. Pan Books: page 49 *tl*. The RAF Museum: page 11. Dieter Rams: page 88 *t*. RCA Ltd: page 45 *ib*. Morphy Richards Ltd: 27 *r*. Rosenthal China (London) Ltd: pages 12, 58 *tl*. De la Rue: page 86. J. Sainsbury's Archives: pages 72 *b*, 83 *m*, 85 *t*. Joseph E Seagram & Sons, Inc (photo. Eztra Stoller): page 55 *l*. Sony: page 27 *l*. The Sunday Times Magazine: page 85 *l*. Tupperware: page 81 *b*. United Nations: page 55 *tr*. UPI/Bettmann: pages 15 *b*, 16/17, 30 *t*, 40 *t*, 41, 48, 73 *b*, 118, 119 *bl br*. Courtesy American VOGUE © 1958 (renewed 1986) by The Condé Nast Publications Inc. (photo. Henry Clarke): page 61 *tl*.

Index